Social Media Marketing 2019

How to Become an Influencer of Millions on Facebook, Twitter, YouTube & Instagram While Advertising & Building Your Personal Brand

Robert Miller

© Copyright 2019 by Robert Miller. All rights reserved.

This document is geared towards providing exact and reliable information regarding topic and issue covered. The publication is sold with the idea that the publisher is not required to render accounting, officially permitted, or otherwise, qualified services. If advice is necessary, legal or professional, a practiced individual in the profession should be ordered.

From a Declaration of Principles which was accepted and approved equally by a Committee of the American Bar Association and a Committee of Publishers and Associations.

In no way is it legal to reproduce, duplicate, or transmit any part of this document in either electronic means or in printed format. Recording of this publication is strictly prohibited and any storage of this document is not allowed unless with written permission from the publisher. All rights reserved.

The information provided herein is stated to be truthful and consistent, in that any liability, in terms of inattention or otherwise, by any usage or abuse of any policies, processes, or directions contained within is the solitary and utter responsibility of the recipient reader. Under no circumstances will any legal responsibility or blame be held against the publisher for any reparation, damages, or monetary loss due to the information herein, either directly or indirectly.

Respective authors own all copyrights not held by the publisher. The information herein is offered for informational purposes solely, and is universal as so. The presentation of the information is without contract or any type of guarantee assurance.

The trademarks that are used are without any consent, and the publication of the trademark is without permission or backing by the trademark owner. All trademarks and brands within this book are for clarifying purposes only and are the owned by the owners themselves, not affiliated with this document.

Table of Contents

Introduction 5

Chapter 1: Social Media's Importance 6

Chapter 2: 2019 Trends 13

Chapter 3: Primary Social Media Platforms 20

Chapter 4: Facebook Marketing 2019 29

Chapter 5: Paid Facebook Marketing 34

Chapter 6: Instagram 2019 60

Chapter 7: Paid Instagram Marketing 79

Chapter 8: YouTube 2019 89

Chapter 9: Paid YouTube Marketing 101

Chapter 10: Twitter 2019 106

Chapter 11: Paid Twitter Marketing 111

Conclusion 115

Introduction

Congratulations on getting a copy of *Social Media Marketing 2019: How to Become an Influencer of Millions on Facebook, Twitter, Youtube & Instagram While Advertising & Building Your Personal Brand.*

The influx of social media platforms over the past 10 years is the greatest boon to marketing since the creation of the internet. While there is undeniably money to be made from social media marketing, the shear amount of competition makes getting started successfully more difficult than it would otherwise be.

That's why this book was created, to provide you with the tools you need to get started off on the right foot. The following chapters will discuss how to do just that, starting with an overview of just what makes social media so important in 2019. Next, you will find a detailed breakdown of many of the social media trends you can expect from 2019 and beyond. You will then find an overview of the social media platforms you should get started on as well as how to choose the best starter option for your brand.

From there, you will find chapters dedicated to paid and free marketing strategies for Facebook, Instagram, YouTube, and Twitter. You will find plenty of suggestions for squeezing as many followers and pageviews as possible out of your chosen platform before learning about the paid options and how to best put them to work for you. Finally, you will find plenty of tips and tricks to ensure your content stands out from the pack.

There are plenty of books on this subject on the market, thanks again for choosing this one! Every effort was made to ensure it is full of as much useful information as possible, please enjoy!

Chapter 1: Social Media's Importance

Let's keep this as simple as possible: your business needs an online presence, and a run of the mill website unfortunately just isn't good enough anymore. In 2019 it doesn't matter what type of business you have, if you don't have a social media presence then you are missing out on free marketing. It is an essential part of any business strategy, and if it's not yet a part of yours, now is the time. While there are a lot of people out there who don't use social media, that number gets smaller and smaller every single day, as more and more people sign up for an account.

The past decade, the landscape of the internet has changed drastically, and most of this change is thanks to social media. As a result, it has become a tool for brands and businesses, opening doors to changing your relationship with the public, engage with your base, and increasing sales.

Every small business starts by, among other things, focusing on getting their first customers. Online businesses often target online shoppers, especially those connected via smartphones and other devices. Others rely on traditional forms of advertising like coupon mailers and print ads. However, while these strategies of hoping customers will find business may work, it is advisable to adapt marketing strategies that will prove successful in the long run. For instance, digital marketing enables businesses of all sizes to reach huge online audiences in a measurable and cost effective manner.

Do keep this in mind: businesses can do well without social media. They can make a profit, and break even. But if you want to continue growing, if you want to constantly be improving sales and making more money, if you want to improve your relationship with your customers and engage with them while at the same time not spending too much money, social media is a great way to do this.

Also, don't forget as more and more of the world gets in social media, more and more people will expect to be able to find their favorite businesses and brands online. They want to communicate with you, to know about their product, and they want to know that you care. Making your customers feel connected to you will help your profits go up because they will feel connected to the product they are buying.

Getting into social media marketing can be tough, and overwhelming. It can feel like a huge, giant project, and often business owners, because of this feeling, decide that it's not worth it. But it is. It is 100 percent worth it as you will be able to more easily interact with prospective clients and find out exactly what they are searching for.

Digital marketing methods are also much cheaper compared to traditional marketing means which enables you to reach a much larger audience at very low costs. You also get to track responses to your marketing efforts which in essence enables you to find out what is working and what you can improve on.

Helps your brand: As you know, your brand is the most valuable thing in your business. Every business is fighting to increase or maintain the visibility of their brand. With a strong brand, you have an edge over your competition. Customers are drawn and tend to be more loyal towards popular brands. With social media, you have an affordable digital marketing method for syndicating content and increasing your business' visibility.

You first come up with a great strategy for social media and engage with a wide audience of potential customers. The social media profiles for your business need to be complete and optimized in order to attract your targeted audience. The best way for increasing brand awareness is through generating content. You must publish posts on the regular and invite people to engage with your content. The "likes" and "shares" will introduce your business to new audiences who will potentially become your customers. The following are some things you can expect social media to do to help you increase brand awareness.

Help you to create visual content: People are more likely to share content that has an image as opposed to text only. So, ensure that you put high quality images in your content.

Showcase your personality: it's important to let your charisma shine through. If you deliver the message in a fun and personable way, people subconsciously drop their guards, and it endears your business to them.

Marketing pays real dividends: Marketing is viewed largely as an expense even though in essence it is an investment. It is a crucial activity especially when it comes to attracting the attention of new customers and prospective clients. You are able to develop services and products demand and eventually turn prospective customers into actual customers. Expanding your social media marketing channels means having a presence in as many media platforms as possible. The more popular ones include Twitter, Facebook, Instagram and YouTube all of which are discussed in detail in later chapters

Improve search engine visibility: Every business wants to be able to increase the amount of user engagement and traffic that they have. But is it really possible to do all of this if your potential customers aren't even able to find you when they go online? There are a number of ways that you are able to increase the potential customers to your site, but having a good social media profile can help you dominate those first search result pages in a natural and organic way, and this in turn, increases the profits that you earn.

When you are thinking about this, you can consider the fact that millennials already spend a ton of time on social platforms, and having your own is going to increase the value of your company more than ever. It cannot only help you to generate more business and profits for yourself, but it can also stop some of the brand negativity it takes to reach top positions.

It acts as the mouthpiece for your company: Whether you have been in the industry for a long time, or you are just starting out, having a positive word of mouth for your business will help you to gain more customers and keep your business running. Social media marketing can be a great way to help you as a business owner interact with your customers and generate positive buzz via word of mouth. You can use it to talk about policies in the company, team activities, new launches, and any other information that is needed for the business.

Social networking online can really help your business because you are given a chance to build up a narrative that you can use to capture the interest of your customers. Each piece of content you created can then be curated in such a way that it shares the values and ethics of the company, along with the product, promoting your business on both ends.

Essential social media marketing plan campaign tools

While a successful social media marketing campaign can bring with it a wide variety of potential benefits, it can only do so if you go into it with the right tools from the start.

A good plan: One of the things that you really need to have is a plan that will support your brand and efforts for many years to come. Such a plan will keep you on track and help you to achieve your marketing ambitions. The plan does not need to be as elaborate as a scientific manual. However, it should be clearly written with a well-defined path and exact steps that need to be taken in order to achieve your business's overall aim. If this plan and strategy are then communicated to your team, then your whole business will soon start reaping the dividends of your extensive and elaborate plans. Likewise, if you are working all alone then having clearly defined goals will make it much more likely that you actually reach them.

An excellent product or service: Any social media marketing or advertising campaigns will not bear fruit if you do not have an excellent product or service to offer your future customers. Excellent products or services are those that solve a problem your customers have while at the same time providing a lasting solution. To achieve this you will need to listen to your customers and take their opinions into consideration.

A presentable brand: Having a professional brand is absolutely essential for your success. A brand is much more than just your company's logo. It entails a lot more including what people get to hear and talk about as well as what they feel and think about your business. Make sure that you put together a budget that will support your efforts in building a powerful brand that will stand out from the crowd.

An excellent pitch: As a business owner, you can expect numerous individuals to ask you over and over again about your business and your products. You need to be ready with quality, interesting answers that will intrigue them. Avoid making the mistake of replying with long, boring answers that will drive your potential customers away. Prepare a pitch and make it interesting, fun, and exciting. Then make sure that you are able to deliver it anytime anyone asks about your business regardless of what online setting you find yourself in

Understand ROI: One of the biggest misconceptions that many business leaders will have about Return on Investment (ROI), is that it pertains to revenue generating actions. Unfortunately, this is far from the truth. ROI pertains mostly to the brand building methods that are more profitable in the long run than the conversion of actual sales due to the ad campaign. Social media is about the process of building customer conversation, and connectivity. It is about using social media outlets to reach those that are not familiar with your brand and helping them to understand your passions as a company.

There are a few metrics that need to be monitored to examine the impact your social media account is having on your ROI. These include:

- Lifetime Value
- Churn
- The overall cost of operation

Lifetime value is a measurement that will calculate the frequency as well as the annual total of purchases for each customer prior to the ad campaign and after the ad campaign. By using the lifetime value as a calculative measure for the ROI you are setting a baseline for the impact that the social media ad campaign is having on your bottom line.

To understand how social media is hurting or improving your customers' loyalty you can check the churn. The churn will tell you how many customers you have gained or lost, as well as the volume by which it went up or down. Next, you will work towards understanding the concept that a dollar that is saved is also a dollar that is earned. It can be quite difficult to measure the ROI of your social media account, however, you can measure the social media's impact that has taken place on the brand's equity, as well as the benefit of the bottom line.

Chapter 2: 2019 Trends

Social media is here to stay, and it looks like it is only going to become even more influential as it continues to evolve and change quickly to keep up with the ever growing demands of society. Experiences will only become more interactive, immersive and influential, and for a business to survive, it must be leveraging the social media experience at every opportunity. Social media marketing is here to stay.

Innovation in marketing in this era is essential. As a business owner, you need to keep yourself updated with some of the latest trends in marketing and advertising. There are quite a number of innovations that will be adapted in 2019 that will help to take your business to the next level. For the foreseeable future at least, especially these are a few important trends to keep tabs on including the increasing importance of influencers, VR and AR, sales enablement, artificial intelligence, and even more personalized content.

Influencers will be more important than ever

Come the yea   cted to
become and ir   *Potential*   dollars.
Given the rise c   latform
channel, this   *Marketing idea*   nd the
millennials hav   lives,
welcoming the   , even
using that powe *to bring up?*   er they
should purchas   boxing
videos or prodι   iencer
shows off the la   l, etc.,
has created a un

The following are some of the reasons why marketers are turning to influencers to promote their products:

- *Influencers have earned their followers' trust:* someone is more likely to buy a product when it's recommended by a person that they trust. An influencer has already earned the trust of their followers and it puts them in a better position to recommend products.
- *Influencers give you access to a targeted audience:* promoting a product to a small niche-audience is much more rewarding than blasting an ad to a crowd who couldn't care less about your product. When you use an influencer, you gain access to a laser-targeted audience who are likely to purchase your product.
- *Relatively inexpensive*: influencers are very affordable as long as you don't go for Hollywood stars and athletes. For instance, micro influencers charge between $200 and $250 for a post, which is a reasonable price considering they are exposing you to thousands of their targeted followers. Some marketers seem to be of the notion that influencers are too expensive when it isn't the case at all.
- *Boosts SEO:* another method of getting strong backlinks to your site is by leveraging social media influencers. When influencers link to your site, it boosts both your domain authority and page authority, which in turn improves SEO.

While it seems as though influencers hit the mainstream relatively recently, it is already an established part of the status quo to the point that well-known influencers are already making thousands of dollars, if not more, for sponsorships and brand associations. As such, if you have already heard of an influencer then odds are you likely can't afford them if you are just starting out. This is where the latest tier of influencers, known as micro-influencers come into play.

Micro-influencers, as the name implies, do not have followers in the millions, or even in the hundreds of thousands, instead, they typically have around 50,000 followers or less. While the numbers may not be as high, the followers that these micro-influencers have tend to be far more committed than those of their larger peers, to the point that a food brand would likely see a better ROI working with a food blogger with 50,000 followers and a reasonable budget than a more famous alternative whose price is 10 times as high.

The trend of drilling down to find even smaller, and more dedicated, followings is only going to increase in 2019 to the point where nano-influencers, those with a max of 10,000 dedicated followers, are going to start becoming relevant as well. Those who are members of these smaller communities tend to be the most dedicated at all which means that if their favorite nano-influencer recommends your brand the conversion rate is typically greater than 50 percent. As these individuals can often be bought for $100 or some free merchandise, the ROI on this type of social media marketing is only going to continue to increase.

What's more, many of these individuals are completely new to the business which means that they are anxious to form long-term partnerships. As they don't require a large budget to work with, you may be in a place to easily lock an individual down early if you find someone that is clearly going to a big hit once they become a bit more well-known.

Virtual and augmented reality: The term Omni-channel originated around customers in order to describe marketing strategies that exist outside the travel and retail sectors. Omni simply means every kind, all, or the whole. Therefore, Omni-channel marketing refers to reaching out to customers and interacting with them across all possible communication channels, though these days there is an increasing focus on AR and VR. Even then, a focus should be placed on budgets so that only the most effective channels are selected.

Businesses are now using mobile cameras in order to improve customer experience. Through both virtual reality and augmented reality, you can promote brand engagement and also make the pre-purchase decision much easier for your customers. The process will almost bring your products to life. Your customers will be able to make life much easier and better for your customers.

Increased sales enablement: Social media is already well-known for being able to make the product discovery phase of shopping easier than ever before. It allows brands to promote their products through a virtually endless array of channels that make it as easy for the customer to make a purchase as possible. This is only going to continue into 2019 as every social media platform continues to trend towards improved enablement of sales in the business funnel.

According to a recent study of 2018 internet trends, more than 50 percent of those polled had discovered a product via social media that they then subsequently purchased within the past month. Of the social media platforms discussed in this book, Instagram is the leading platform that led to these types of conversions.

Now is the time to take advantage of this trend and get your brand into a position where it can benefit by improving your social strategy. This also means that you will not always need a sales pitch in all of your messaging if you want people to trust you. Instead, social media is making it easier than ever to help you to tell your story and to improve your odds of consideration.

Artificial intelligence: Automated bots have already begun to show up as part of the customer service options for many brands and this type of artificial intelligence is only going to become more common across all social media platforms in 2019. Social media has made it easier than ever for customers to talk to their favorite brands directly and, while this is great in some respects, it also means general expectations for support response times are decreasing.

Chatbots are a natural way to solve this problem while still providing what appears to be personalized customer service. While not all customers are going to be comfortable using chatbots at first, as the adoption rate improves more and more people are sure to get on board once they interact with a few of then and understand their limitations.

What's even better is that the influx of interest in this type of technology means that the responses that these customer service programs can provide are going to become more and more real to the point that most people won't know when they are texting with a real person and when they are talking to a machine. This can take several forms including giving them more personality or simply predicting the types of questions customers are going to ask and writing more detailed responses to cater to every possibility.

AI is also becoming increasing prevalent when it comes to automated messaging to common voiced questions. More and more brands are staffing their customer service centers with messaging that can keep the customer satisfied while at the same time saving money and preventing a person from having to answer the same question dozens of times per day.

Increase emphasis on stories: Stories are becoming more prevalent for brands of all shapes and sizes. This type of vertical, visual content started on Snapchat and was eventually copied by Instagram before moving to Facebook, YouTube and beyond where it has taken the mainstream by storm and will continue to do so into 2019. As of January 2019, there are more than 500 million people consuming stories in one form or another each day which means that harnessing this power effectively is key to remaining relevant in 2019.

Stories are so effective because they allow brands to spark real conversations with their followers in a way that feels organic. As the algorithms that power modern social media platforms become more and more decisive it is no longer enough for brands to encourage followers to like, follow and subscribe, more personal connections are needed. This is going to become increasingly important in 2019 as additional new types of engagement come to the fore, leaving older options left in the dust.

Micro-moment marketing: Micro-moment marketing is all about the changing nature of consumer behavior in the context of their own digital (especially mobile-based) behavior as well as the fact that they are facing information overload as they spend so much time online.

It's based on the idea that consumers today can basically access the "best" of anything in the space of a few seconds--and some 96 percent of consumers will be doing this with their smartphones in the space of a few seconds.

The challenge that this poses to brands and marketers is that now they must be able to essentially "find" their customer in the space of these few moments without having any relevant information about them ahead of time. Thus, businesses must be able to offer more in the way of "one-touch" offerings to accommodate this behavior, build brand loyalty, and stay ahead of their competition.

Traditional marketing is an interruption – if you come "at" them, they're going to be annoyed. But they can choose to come and find you when they need something. So, in the sense that consumers have so many choices available "in the moment," the marketing game has changed. Highly personalized "smart content" that's focused on relationship-building is one response to this, essentially finding a way to address very specific buyer personas. This can be tailored towards a specific characteristic of a demographic, including age, location or even what point in the buyer's journey a person is.

Chapter 3: Primary Social Media Platforms

A big part of successfully rolling out your own social media marketing plan is targeting the right platforms to ensure that your efforts are reaching the greatest portion of your audience as possible. While you will likely want to end up expanding to all of the platforms outlined below, you will want to put your efforts into getting one up and running at a time to ensure you can start seeing the benefits of your efforts as soon as possible.

Factors to consider when choosing a starter social media platform for business purposes include

Cost: The first social network that you work with should be one that has plenty of free advertising options as you will want to avoid paid options until you get a better idea of what works and what does not. If you have to pay to be on social media, then it may not be worth it in the short-term. There are lots of free advertising options for each of the major social media platforms, it is just a matter of determining which seem as though they will work most effectively for you.

Suitability for small businesses: It is important to choose an option that you know you can keep up in the long-term. Starting a social media profile and then leaving it untended is worse than not having one at all. Not having an account is a choice that can be defended, having a poorly curated account shows that you don't care about your online appearance and can be enough turn some people away right from the start.

Popularity for your niche: There are two types of thought when it comes to the best type of platform to choose. You can either choose one that is popular with other small businesses in your niche, or you can go the other way and go with a lesser picked option. On one hand, you know that people interested in your niche will be on the platform and looking to engage in content, but you risk being lost in the crowd. On the other hand, you will be able to stand out more easily, but you don't know if there is going to be anybody looking. Neither option is superior to the other as long as you know what you are getting into.

Ease of use: It is important to have an idea of what type of content you are going to be creating the most of as you will want to ensure the primary platform you choose is one that you won't have to fight with every time you want to create a post.

Advanced features: You are able to achieve a lot more an engage your customers and followers better on social networks with advanced features.

Geographic targeting: Most small businesses have a local focus so the ability to target a specific niche of the market or particular geographic area adds lots of value.

Age: There are some social networks that are more popular with certain age groups. For instance, Instagram is more popular with millennials while Facebook is suitable for people of all ages.

Facebook

Facebook is an incredibly powerful marketing tool that is essential for any successful small business owner to take advantage of. Businesses who are not actively using Facebook in some way, shape, or form are robbing themselves of untold profits. It continues to be one of the leading social networking platforms, making it a huge tool for accessing your target market and increasing your sales.

Here are some of the reasons why you need to be taking advantage of Facebook for marketing your business:

A massive number of active users: The sheer size of Facebook's active users alone should be enough to encourage any company to lay down roots on the Facebook network. Facebook has more than 1 billion active users visiting its site on a daily basis, and more than 2 billion active monthly visitors. This means that on a daily basis you are tapping into a market that accounts for 1/7 to 2/7 of the entire global population. The reach is massive, making it a highly valuable tool for marketers to use.

Evenly split demographics: Every network has its demographic audience, but almost none stack up to Facebook. Facebook is unique in a sense that it has a very evenly split demographic. It's users are a strong balance of men and women from nations all across the globe. With this balance, that means it is almost a given that your niche will be hanging out on Facebook ready to consume your content!

Global network: Facebook has a strong North American presence, but it actually has an incredibly strong international presence as well. India, Brazil, and Indonesia account for a great deal of the active daily audience after the US. This means that you can expand your target audience far beyond the core and capitalize in a far bigger way using Facebook.

Language translation: Something that regularly holds people back from being able to conduct business across borders is language barriers. Not being able to communicate with international audience's in a language they understand can ultimately hinder your ability to sell overseas. Not anymore, though! Facebook has more than 70 translations available on its platform meaning that users from all around the world can read your page and purchase anything you may be selling.

Instagram

Instagram is extremely popular with people under 30, them making up 59 percent of the platform, and people under 25 use Instagram for an average of 32 minutes a day. In terms of teenagers, 72 percent of them use Instagram every day, second only to Snapchat, and since Instagram has put in a story option similar to Snapchat's formula, that number is getting higher. This is an extremely valuable tool if your product is more aimed towards that generation.

If you want your business to be picked up internationally, 80 percent of Instagram users are outside the US. This is especially valuable if your product is something that can be ordered or used online, like a course or a blog. If you're located in a tourist town, this is also a thing to consider.

YouTube

YouTube originally made itself known with cat videos and wacky, obscure content, but now it is the world's second largest search engine, second only to Google. There are over a billion users, nearly a third of everyone on the internet, and every day billions of hours of video are consume. YouTube can be navigated in 76 different languages, that is 95 percent of everyone on the internet, and it is the second most visited website in the world.

Google prioritizes video content in its search results, especially video coming from YouTube. Website pages with video are 53 times more likely to rank highly on Google searches. It is plain to see why YouTube is a cut above other video sharing services with those statistics alone. If you want to get your name out there, it will go a long way towards helping you. However, why should you care about getting your name out there?

If you are a creative person, the answer might seem obvious, because you enjoy creating content whether makeup tutorials or video game streams and sharing it. But, if you are a business, the answer might be more difficult to see initially.
The beauty of YouTube for business is that it gives you a chance to get personal with your audience and gain their trust. For instance, say you run a small physical therapy business. You could produce videos on how to do a variety of exercises, thus setting yourself up as an authority on the matter and hopefully pulling in more customers.

It may seem counter-intuitive to teach your audience what you want them to buy from you, but once they start learning from you, they will trust you and see the value you offer, making them more likely to use your business in the future.
YouTube also allows you to interact with your audience and customers. Try asking them questions in your videos, or if you notice people asking the same question frequently, you can make a video answering that question.

You can comment on other people's channels, getting your name across their screen, which they will hopefully click if you are compelling. If you build that bond viewers become loyal, and it will also help you better understand who your audience is, thus making you able to market yourself better.

Creating your own YouTube channel is as easy as creating a Google account which is to say that if you already have some type of Google account then you already have a YouTube channel waiting for you. To activate it, all you need to do is to log into your Google account as normal before heading to YouTube.com and looking for the choice listed as My Channel. Clicking on this option will allow you to name your page and doing so will officially create it. When it comes to choosing a name for your page, the first thing you are going to want to do is to determine what type of content you are going to create and then choose a name that is relevant to that type of content. You will also then want to add in keywords and phrases that are related to the type of content you ultimately decided to produce.

Decide on content: If you aren't interested in creating content that personally means something to you, and are instead more concerned with appealing to the widest variety of advertisers, then you are likely going to want to consider creating product review videos. Essentially, these are going to be short (3 minutes maximum) videos that break down a product's relative strengths and weakness and they are extremely popular and can be targeted at a specific audience with ease. As such, you are going to want to choose an audience that is specific enough that it can easily be targeted by marketers.

This means you are going to want to focus on a segment of the market that has disposable income and a hobby or interest that is never going to be at a loss for new products. The best case scenario is to find a niche with a wide margin of product prices as you are going to have to purchase every item you review, at least until you start getting some clout in your niche. If you can make your channel all about reviewing the cheap end of an expensive hobby, then you can target those types of advertisers looking to pull in the big fish without spending an arm and a leg yourself.

Add content: After you have created your account and determined what types of videos you are going to be creating on the regular, the next thing you are going to need to do is to actually start creating content. If you are unsure of what a good product review video looks like, simply search for a review of a product you are already familiar with so you know what is being discussed.

When it comes to ensuring views, the best way to do so is to encourage viewers to subscribe to your channel and the best way to do that is to post quality content on a regular basis. You are going to want to start off by posting between 15 and 20 videos and then post at least two new entries every week. This way you will provide potential subscribers with enough relevant and quality content that they feel justified in being notified each time you post a new video. Additionally, you will want to ensure that each video is labeled and tagged appropriately so that those in your chosen niche will be able to find it with even the most generic niche related searches.

Profit: Once your new videos are regularly generating at least 1,000 views per video you will know that you have enough of a subscriber base to begin to successfully monetize your page. Luckily, the key to doing so is already built into your channel through what is known as the monetization tab. This tab can be found in the options menu and it will let YouTube start placing relevant advertisements before your videos. You will also want to connect your channel to Google AdSense which, in turn, will turn on various advertisements based on each viewer's browser history. More information on AdSense can be found at Google.com/AdSense.

Both of these types of advertisements will start out with a pay per click structure, though if you reach enough subscribers you will eventually gain access to pay per view advertisements as well. If you plan on making money in this fashion it is important to never use copyrighted material in your videos. A pay per click structure typically pays out 20 cents per click, with 1,000 views being enough to assume 10 people will actually click on the advertisement in question. If you gain enough of a following to qualify for pay per view type ads, then you can expect to make roughly $3 for every 1,000 views the ad receives.

This is why YouTube affiliate marketing is such a numbers game as it is practically impossible to create only a small number of videos that return the type of views that are required to generate anything remotely resembling a reliable revenue stream. Instead, you are going to want to create as many videos as possible, especially as your subscriber base initially takes off. This is because the internet is inherently fickle, which means you will want to capitalize on any moments of popularity that you do experience as you never know how long they are going to last.

Twitter

This platform is great for some businesses but not for all. This is why you need to understand the different types of social media. Twitter is awesome for mini posts and sharing links to blog posts and articles. The platform is designed to allow users to post short messages known as tweets. However, you can also post links, images, videos, polls, and much more.

Twitter is ideal for businesses that target a tech-savvy audience, elites, intellects who love brief but precise messages and information in bit-sized chunks. Keep in mind that this is the world's third largest social media platform so doing well here can be a huge blessing. As a business owner, you should set up a Twitter business page and start reaching out to customers and other members on the platform. When you do, you will be able to gain a presence and thereby establish a brand identity.

The ideal posts to share include business information, launches and events, time-sensitive updates, shout-outs, and to re-tweet other people's posts. It is advisable to post between one and three times each day to the more than 275 million monthly visitors.

To create an account on Twitter, simply go to the Twitter for Business page and then simply sign up. Once your account is up and running, you should start following major brands, influential individuals, as well as users within your niche. You should also begin posting updates and providing links to useful content and helpful articles. Re-tweeting is also highly advisable so re-tweet any content that you find interesting, catchy, exciting and so on. Remember that there are customers out there who rely on platforms such as Twitter to communicate with brands and receive customer service.

If you have a very visible brand or perhaps you do not own a blog, then you may wish to skip this platform. Please note, however, that there are numerous companies that thrive on this platform. This is because of their unique products and brand as well as a distinct voice. Try and set yourself apart so that you stand out among the rest. Companies thrive on Twitter when they engage their customers and listen as they express themselves and share their concerns.

Chapter 4: Facebook Marketing 2019

How many people do you currently know who are NOT on Facebook? The answer you've most likely given is – no one. Because everyone is on Facebook. Billions of people from around the globe hold a Facebook social media account and that is exactly why existing businesses and prospective businesses should get online and get on Facebook (if they haven't already done so). Not only are those billions of people connected on this social media platform, but they log in multiple times in a day just to either check what's happening or to post an update themselves. For a business, that's almost a billion people a day, multiple times a day who could potentially see your product or service.

With features such as page insights, content, page and ad management, content curation and more, Facebook is a social media marketing goldmine for businesses. And the best part of this is setting up a basic page for a business is free! Some features on Facebook require you to pay a small fee, but the unbeatable low price that the social media platform is quoting is a lot lower than it would cost to market the conventional way.

One of the biggest challenges faced by business users of Facebook and other social media platforms who are using these as marketing tools are getting their followers to become paying customers. Gathering a large following on a Facebook page is one step. The next step is converting those followers into paying customers which can only be done with a lot of patience.

Social media is a constantly changing environment. Information just keeps coming in one after another and it's evident by how quickly items appear on a Facebook newsfeed. When it comes to marketing on social media platforms like Facebook, businesses need to be patient. Remember that it's Facebook, and users lose interest and get distracted quickly. What you need to do as a business is to keep their attention, and hold on to it long enough to change their minds about buying from your business. This chapter will focus on the free opportunities Facebook offers when it comes to advertising

Become an authority

In order to attract the type of readers that are interested in the content you are peddling, the best way to do this reliably is to start posting content on a regular basis and then never stop. During the early days, it is important to keep posting regularly, using appropriate SEO, even if you aren't getting any hits. You are going to need a backlog of content regardless, so keep at it and don't lose faith in the process.

In many situations, the word expert and the word authority are often used interchangeably; this is not the case with sales, however, as being an authority is everything and being an expert is much worse than simply getting second place. In this case, an expert is someone who knows a lot about a certain niche while an authority is the person that all of the experts agree is the first stop for information. To put it another way, authorities aren't authorities because they say they are, they are authorities because when they make declarations in regard to their niche of choice, other people listen.

The benefits of being an authority for your chosen niche are much the same as being an authority in any other situation when you speak, other people listen. This is because those who know you are an authority are naturally going to assume you know what you are talking about for a given situation. It doesn't take much to see how this can translate directly into additional conversions when given a little extra push. If you can reach the status of authority for your niche, then you will be able to set the tone for the niche as a whole, along with legions of fans that will be willing to automatically agree with whatever you say.

During this period, you are going to want to seek out the online spaces that people interested in your niche tend to congregate and become a fixture in them. This means competing blogs, YouTube channels, subreddits, essentially wherever the audience you are targeting goes, they need to see you. During this phase, it is important to only include links to your posts occasionally, as you want people to engage in your content and not get turned off because they think it is a marketing ploy. Instead of focusing on marketing, focus on providing your target audience with useful information and before long they will start seeking you out.

Once your name begins to get out there, you can then move on to capturing the attention of the other experts in the niche. Any expert can offer up their opinion, the authority in a given niche is the one that the other experts seek out as well. This means that you will want to eventually reach out to the creators of the niche blogs you have been frequenting and offer to contribute to their blog. As long as you provide links to your own content which shows you are an expert, many bloggers will be happy to not have to generate a post for once and take you up on your offer. Once your name starts showing up on other niche websites, you know you are one your way to becoming an authority.

Once you start driving traffic to your site directly from competing blogs, the next thing you are going to want to do is to use the outline you wrote when you were becoming an expert and expand it into a full eBook. Writing a 5,000-word book on the niche in question should come easily to you at this point, and you can put the whole thing together by yourself and even post it to the Amazon Kindle Marketplace, all for free. You then give the book away in exchange for signing up for the email newsletter that you will want to set up, in an effort to start collecting information on your readers in an effort to market to them more effectively. The regular visitors to your page are likely to sign up, putting them in the prime spot for the marketing of products targeted to those with a clearly defined group of interests.

Create Facebook Groups

Help your customers: The second type of Facebook groups is dedicated to acquired customers. To build this community, invite people to join the group as soon as they make a purchase. Make customers aware of the existence of the group and that you would like them if they too registered.

Explain how the group works in the "information" section. For example, members can get to know each other, share ideas and strategies and help each other in any way. Be sure to send an email with the link to subscribe to the group and monitor who signs up or not. Do not forget to invite people who have not yet registered several times.

Here are some ways to develop your group on Facebook:

Be generous and promote a "give" policy: For example, offer tips or tricks to use the lesser known features of your product and invite other users to share their findings. You could invite members of your fan group to share tips and tricks with them too.

Be transparent: Respond personally to customer criticism. For example, thank the customer who makes you notice the flaw in your product and respond that you will immediately fix it. It is not necessary to promise discounts or promotions to the disgruntled customer, but it is important to thank him for the report, to apologize and to promise that he will be contacted when the problem is solved.

Be present: Answer questions and comments as soon as possible. If you cannot give an immediate answer, still let your customer know that you will respond quickly.

Be inclusive: Offer group members promotions and offers that are not on the official page. Make your customers feel part of an exclusive club.

Chapter 5: Paid Facebook Marketing

Creating a great campaign with Facebook Ads can seem a little bit overwhelming in the beginning, but there are so many great things that you can do when you utilize all the features that come with it. While you do need to think about the ad itself, you must make sure you understand the platform that you are using. Once you determine who you're trying to target, and you have a good idea of how much you want to spend on the campaign, then it is easier to focus on some of the smaller details.

You need to make sure that from the beginning you set up a budget and a bid strategy for your campaign. Otherwise, you will keep the campaign going way too long and you will end up spending more than you intended. Facebook has made this part easy though with the use of Optimized CPM.

With this kind of tool, you are giving Facebook the permission it needs to bid for ad space based on any goals or constraints that you provide to it. This is often the best way for you, especially as a beginner, to maximize your budget and avoid any overspending. Until you are able to get an idea of how much the ad space costs, and how to best allocate your budget, just stick with the Optimized CPM to get the most out of your campaign.

A Facebook ad campaign has three levels. At the top is the Campaign, then the Ad Set, and then the Ad itself. At the campaign level, you will choose an objective or goal like "Increase Sales" or "Increase Total Likes for my Business Facebook Page." At the Ad Set level, you will set your budget, your schedule, your target audience, and your ad placement. Once you have chosen the parameters of your ad set, you will design your ad or multiple ads to be run with the same ad set. Your ad set may contain one or more ads, and the ads must be individual creations that contain text, video, images, and/or links. Your ad set is what will attract attention to your business or brand and will help you achieve both your short-term and long-term goals.

Facebook Ads vs Boosted Posts: Which Should You Choose?

This question is very common among the admins of Facebook pages. Even if you are new to a page, you are bound to see Facebook's prompt to 'boost a post' and this usually comes in when Facebook detects high activity on a certain post or if its algorithms have found other pages with similar content boosting a certain type of content that matches yours. The ability to boost your post is a very simplified addition to Facebook Ads system. This system is designed to be simple and easy to use even for a non-marketer or advertiser. However, simple doesn't always mean better. Boosted posts come at the cost of significant customization the complete ad system provides.

What have boosted posts on Facebook?

With boosted posts, advertisers have the choice to use a post that has already been posted at any time and promote it. When boosting a post, page admins can choose their target audience, decide on a budget and how long the boosted post should run. This can be done on any post on your page's timeline.

Facebook Ads vs boosted posts: A post that is boosted focuses on increased visibility for that particular post and in an effort to increase engagement as much as possible. Boosted posts are great for brand awareness and an increase in engagement can be value added for social proof. An increase in engagement can also mean a lower CPC (cost-per-click) or CPA (cost-per-acquisition), you also could end up with more results with the same value of the investment.

With Facebook's recent update, you not only can increase engagement for that particular post, but you can also choose the outcome of it- whether you want people to visit your profile more or visit your site. If this is your option, compared to increasing engagement on the post in terms of likes or comments, your ad be visible to people who will most likely end up clicking. This option is available only if your boosted post has a link to it.

Step one – Determine your goals

The first step towards creating an effective ad campaign structure is to set firm and clear goals, and then to allocate each goal to an individual campaign. Then, every ad set and the ad will be oriented towards your chosen objectives - no matter how big or small, how long-term or how short term. For example, your objective may be something like increasing the number of installs your app has, increasing overall traffic to your website, increasing sales of a particular item, or simply to generate more "Likes" for your Facebook business page.

Tip #1: *Limit one objective per advertisement, that way you can tailor your audience and budget to achieve maximum value from your ad campaign.*

Tip #2: *Get creative! If your objective is to increase Page Likes, consider designing an ad that offers a 10% discount code to anyone who Likes and Follows your business Facebook page. While this would work well for increasing Facebook Page Likes, offering 10% off for a Facebook Like may not generate more website traffic, since your website is not directly involved. This is why we recommend limiting your objectives to one objective per ad.*

Step two - Define your audience

The second step is to allocate your ad sets to the audiences you most want to target. One ad set might be aimed at Men, age 18 to 24, while another ad set might aim at Women, age 18 to 24. It is important to allocate different ad sets to different audiences so that your ad sets do not end up competing with one other. It also important to keep your target audience in mind when designing each ad set. Men may be more likely to stop and look at an ad that includes a scantily-clad model in it, but most women will probably scroll right past - or worse, they may block the ad.

The proper ad campaign structure is crucial for any business, small or large, and any brand, whether that brand supports a single product or many products. With a well-formed, thoughtfully-designed ad campaign, your company could see an increase in website or social media traffic, an increase in profits, improved brand recognition, and so much more!

An effective campaign structure is the first step in a successful ad campaign, as it will help you to set specific goals for specific campaigns, measure the results of those campaigns, discover which campaigns are working and which are not, and allocate your budget in the most effective way possible. It will also help you to create multiple ad sets for multiple audiences so that you can determine who is most likely to generate business for your company or brand. Through variations in image, text, links, and videos, a properly structured campaign will even allow you to see what types of ads are having the biggest impact on your audience.

Facebook can help you build your audience. Facebook Ads Manager separates the different types of audience into three categories: Core Audiences, Custom Audiences, and Lookalike Audiences.

Facebook Ads Manager allows you to manually narrow down your Core Audience by the following factors:

Location: There are four options which shape the scope of your audience targeting.

- Everyone (for everyone in a given area)
- Locals (those that claim the area as "home")
- New Residents (those who have recently updated the area as "home")
- Visitors (those have recently "checked in" to this location, or nearby locations)

The "given area" can be the narrowed down by your zip code, and can even include neighboring zip codes if you are looking for a broader reach. The location of your audience is important to consider, as not every business is looking for tourists and not every business is looking for locals. For example a hotel would want to target visitors and tourists, whereas a bakery will want to target local residents.

Consider location carefully before making a decision about which locations or areas to include in your campaign. If you are advertising a product that can be shipped outside of your state, or outside of your country, then you will want the location to be very broad. However, if you are advertising a specific service, you may only want to advertise in the area that you are willing to provide this service.

For example: If your business is a Maid service, you may only want to advertise within the sixty square miles of your home or business. It probably would not make sense to advertise your Maid service hundreds of miles away.

Demographics: Facebook allows marketers to target specific age ranges, specific genders, and specific spoken languages.

- Age Ranges: while a hotel would want to target all age ranges, a tattoo parlor may only want to target people under the age of 40. Be sure to choose an age range that suits your product or business.
- Genders: again, while a hotel may want to target all genders, a hair salon may only want to target women. 90% of the time, you will want to target both men and women, so consider very carefully before choosing to exclude either gender.
- Languages: if the staff at your business speak more than language, it is important to advertise this. For example, if your business is based in Southwest Arizona, and you (or a staff member) are fluent in Spanish, as well as English, advertise to both English-speaking and Spanish-speaking customers.

Interest: Targeting by interest allows marketers to reach people based on what they have listed as their interests and activities on their Facebook profile, the posts and comments that they have "liked" on Facebook, and the posts and comments that they have created. For example, if your business makes customized dog collars, Facebook Ads Manager will target users who have dogs, follow dog- or pet-related pages, or have dogs listed as an interest in their profile.

Behavior: Targeting by behavior allows marketers to reach people based on what they buy, what kinds of devices they use, whether they are using a desktop to access Facebook or a mobile phone, and other similar factors. For example, if you are advertising your new iPhone app, Facebook Ads Manager will target users who access Facebook via their iPhone or other Apple-branded product. After all, iPhone apps are only available for iPhones and cannot be used across other mobile phone platforms or operating systems.

Connections: Targeting by connections allows marketers to select their audience based on their connections to pages, apps, or events. It also allows you to target the friends of people connected to pages and apps. Example: if your business is a bakery, you can target audience members that have liked other bakeries in your area.

Audience size: Be aware that with every factor you use to narrow your audience, your target audience may become very small. This is where it is important to consider including zip codes beyond your own. Be sure to pay close attention to the Audience Size Indicator provided by the Facebook Ads Manager, to make sure you are not spending a large amount of your budget on a very small or narrow audience.

Custom Audiences: Custom Audiences are audiences built on your own data, as opposed to the Core Audiences which are based solely on Facebook's data. Custom Audience sources can come from data files (from your Point of Sale system, your email lists, or your client database). Custom Audience sources can also come from website data (data collected from your company's website), mobile app data (data collected from your company's mobile apps), or Facebook data (data collected from people's interactions with your Facebook page, ads, and videos).

Make sure your data sources coincide with your goals. For example, if you are looking to ==drive up sales and increase revenue, you should be targeting frequent shoppers and high-value clients==.

It is also important to ensure that the proper devices have been targeted. For instance, if your audience tends to shop more via mobile phone, your targeting should reflect this. Use complete and up-to-date data for the best results. If you are using an email list to generate your audience, make sure that email list is up-to-date, and not riddled with old email accounts that are no longer in use. Using old information will only result in your ad budget being wasted.

You can also use your Custom Audience data to target customers based on their previous interactions with your business.

- If a customer has made a prior purchase, you could advertise complementary products.
- Re-market old products to members of your audience that have already encountered your message.
- Use Custom Audiences to upsell.
- Use Custom Audiences to show new customers that they have friends or connections that like your business or use your product or service.

Facebook uses a security process called "data hashing," which heavily encrypts your data. Facebook's data hashing has been reviewed by an independent third party, Pricewaterhouse Coopers, and they have confirmed that your data is secure - from the implementation of your data to the storage of your data. So, you need not worry that the audience information you share or the payment information you provide is vulnerable to cyber threats. While no system can ever be 100% secure, Facebook's data hashing severely limits the actual threat to your information.

Lookalike audiences: Lookalike Audiences are people who have similar online traits to your current customer base. There are three types of Lookalike Audiences: Value-Based Lookalikes, International Lookalikes, and Multi-Country Lookalikes.

Value-Based Lookalikes: When creating a Custom Audience, you can create a customer value file which will help you find new customers who are similar to your highest spending, or high-value, clients. For example, if many of your high-value clients are considered "upper class," you may want to target an audience that frequents expensive local restaurants or local golf clubs. When creating a Value-Based Lookalike audience in Facebook Ads Manager, it is important that stereotypes exist for a reason, and stereotypes can definitely be used to your advantage in terms of marketing and advertising.

International Lookalikes: For a company to expand across the globe, Lookalike Audiences can target those who most resemble your customer base in any country - not just in one particular region. This is especially valuable if your company provides goods with international shipping options.

Multi-Country Lookalikes: Target a region, such as Europe or North America, and market across multiple countries at the same time. This is especially valuable if your business is located near another country. For example, if your business is located in northern Michigan, targeting audience members in Canada may be beneficial, as they may be willing to cross the border if your services are of particular interest to them.

To create a Lookalike Audience, you must first create a Seed Audience. This is a sample of at least one hundred of your best customers - those that are heavily engaged in your online content, or those who make the largest or most valuable purchases. The more people in your Seed Audience, the better Facebook can help find Lookalike audiences.

Seed Audiences can be created from Custom Audiences, from data collected from your website and/or mobile app, and from the data collected from your Facebook pages. When creating a Lookalike Audience, it is important to consider your end goal. Are you looking for a new audience similar to your existing audience? Or are you looking to broaden your overall reach by adding to your existing audience?

When choosing your audience size in the Facebook Ads Manager, know that if your audience size is closer to "one," you will get a smaller but more similar audience to your current seed audience. If the audience size number in the Facebook Ads Manager is closer to "ten," you will get a larger, broader audience, but it may contain fewer (if any) similarities to that of your seed audience.

Once you have saved your Core Audience, Custom Audience, and Lookalike Audience, you can access them for future ad campaigns in the Facebook Ads Manager. You can also alter their parameters in the event that overlap between your various audiences lowers the delivery of your ad sets.

If you have multiple ad sets targeting similar audiences during the same period of time, then your ad sets might end up competing with each other in the ad auction. This can drive up prices and lead to an inefficient or ineffective use of your budget.

Know your budget: When you allocate your audience, you will also be at the point in ad set design where you will get to determine how to allocate your budget and the different aspects of budgeting you will need to keep in mind. The first two aspects of budgeting to consider are Daily Budget and Lifetime Budget.

- Daily Budget: the amount you are willing to spend on an ad set per day.

- Lifetime Budget: the amount you are willing to spend on an ad set in total.

Facebook Ads Manager also provides two specialty buying options, Reach & Frequency and Target Rating Points.

- **Reach & Frequency:** This specialty buying option is ideal if your campaign needs to target more than 200,000 people. It provides controlled ad delivery at a locked price. For more information, visit the Facebook Business page at https://www.facebook.com/business/learn/facebook-reach-and-frequency-buying

- **Target Rating Points:** This specialty buying option allows you to purchase video ads on Facebook, much like you would if you were purchasing television ads on a national network. For more information, visit the Facebook Business FAQ page at https://www.facebook.com/business/help/518993728299293

Facebook ad campaigns can cost you as little as $5.00 a week, or as much as $50,000 a week. This aspect is highly customizable. Once a budget is set, the Facebook Ad Manager will automatically calculate the "audience reach," based on your budget and the length of time you have chosen to run the campaign. If you want your ad to reach a wider audience, you can either increase your budget or reduce the length of your ad campaign.

The Ads Manager will also calculate the cost per result for you. If you, or your client, want to set a budget based on the cost per result (instead of a budget based on the campaign as a whole), this calculation is the one you will need to look at most closely.

In addition, Facebook Ads Manager allows to tailor your budget even further in the following ways:

- Campaign Spending Limit: This parameter allows you to set the maximum amount you are willing to spend on the advertising campaign in question. This is your overall budget for a SINGLE ad.
- Account Spending Limit: This parameter allows you to set a maximum amount you are willing to spend on ALL of your campaigns, not just one particular ad.

Given the specific requirements of your advertising campaign, like the budget, bid, or targeted audience, the Ads Manager will give you an estimate how many people your advertisement will reach before you actually publish the ad. This is especially useful if you or your client are unsure about your budget or audience.

Once your ad campaign has been published, you will receive performance updates throughout the campaign. These results are available on the "Insights" tab in the Ads Manager. It is very important to take these updates into consideration throughout the campaign, as adjustments to the campaign parameters may be necessary to hit your performance goals - like increasing your budget, or reducing or expanding your audience.

If, for some reason, your ad campaign is completely unsuccessful, and Facebook Ads Manager is unable to obtain the results that were quoted to you when the ad was published - whether the issue is related to your budget or your ad strategy - Facebook Ads Manager will stop delivering the ad and you will not be charged if you did not receive results. This "guarantee" is especially important for first-time advertisers and small business owners that have a tight advertising budget.

Once your budget has been set, the Facebook Ads Manager will spread your Lifetime Budget out over the entire length of your ad campaign. Doing so may cause your Daily Budget to decrease, but Facebook Ads Manager will never exceed the Daily Budget you originally set. This ensures you that Facebook Ads Manager never goes "over-budget" on any aspect of your campaign and that you never spend more money than you are willing to spend on an ad campaign.

Tip: Set a cap on your expenditures, track how much money you have spent using Facebook's spend meters, and measure your campaign's performance using the ads reporting tab in the Facebook Ads Manager.

Tip: Avoid changing your budget type mid-campaign. Doing so will reset your budget, and this may alter the ad analysis provided by Facebook Ads manager. Also, you can use the Audience Insight feature in Ads Manager to help with your target selection.

Step three

The third step is to bid for your various objectives. For example, let us say that your chosen objective was to direct traffic to your website. In that case, Facebook Ads Manager will charge you when your ad is delivered to an audience that is most likely to click the provided link, which will then direct them to your website. You will not be charged when the link is clicked, but you will be charged each time the ad is shown to someone who has a proven history of following the links provided in advertisements. This is important because it prevents you from being charged if the same person clicks on your link repeatedly, which can happen by mistake or as a result of a malicious intent to abuse and misuse your ad campaign.

At this stage, you will also choose where you would like your ad to be placed on the Facebook platform. Ads may be displayed in the desktop News Feed, the mobile News Feed, or in the column to the right (outside of the News Feed). Displaying your ad in the column to right could be beneficial, as those ads are typically stationary and do not scroll away as the user scrolls up and down through their News Feed. Advertising in that right-hand column can generate more attention, or more consistent attention, from Facebook users. On the other hand - displaying your ad here may not provide greater attention, as many Facebook users rarely let their eyes divert away from their actual News Feed. There is no guarantee, so you may want to try a different ad campaign in each location, just to see what will work best for your ad sets and your business.

==When choosing your ad location, take your demographics and target audience into serious consideration.==

For example - should an ad be shown in the desktop News Feed or the mobile News Feed if the target audience is between 18 and 24 years of age? It should probably appear in the mobile News Feed, as this age group is much more likely to access Facebook on their mobile phones than on an actual computer.

Or - should an ad be shown in the desktop News Feed or the mobile News Feed if the target audience is between 65 and 80 years of age? It should probably appear in the desktop News Feed, as this age group probably does not access Facebook on their mobile phones, and if they do, they may find it difficult to read or interact with your ad set on such a small screen.

Tip: *Choose multiple placement options to give your ads the best chance of engagement.*

Tip: *If you believe that one ad set is performing better than another, change just one of the ad settings, like: bidding, budget, placement, or targeting. Keep all other settings the same. This will reveal which setting is having the most impact, allowing you to learn more about the demographics connected to your business brand, what works, and what does not work.*

Step four

The fourth step is to create a variety of ads and see which of those ads work best for your goals. You can use a combination of text, links, images, and video, and you can use up to fifty different ads in any given ad set. If one ad, in particular, is performing poorly, you can easily turn that ad off without altering or stopping the rest of your ad campaign, and without upsetting your budget. Best of all - Facebook Ads Manager never charges you for stopping or altering your ad campaign.

Keep in mind that your ads need to be eye-catching, otherwise audience members will scroll right past them without ever looking at what you have to present.

- *Video Ads*: keep the video short and make sure any audio attached to the video is neither too loud nor too quiet. Studies show that most people will click away from any ad video that lasts longer than twenty seconds.
- *Image Ads*: keep the images small enough to display nicely on a cell phone screen, and try to include some text on or around the image. Without the text, many audience members may be unsure of what it is you are advertising or what your objective is.

Another important thing to keep in mind when designing your ads is copyright laws. Be extremely careful with the images and videos that you use. Take advantage of websites like Shutterstock.com, whether you can safely purchase images or videos that are relevant to your product, brand, or company. Or, better yet, take the photos or film the videos yourself!

If your ad includes an image or video that you found via a quick Google search, and you did not obtain the appropriate copyright release, the owner of that image or video could allege theft, could send a "Cease & Desist" letter that would require you to stop using the image or video, and could even sue you and collect some of the profits that you saw as a result of the ad campaign their image or video was used in. Copyright laws are surprisingly strict, and if there is a copyright dispute, it can be a very st[...]

Similar [...] roperty laws," which a[...] Be careful with what yo[...] make sure the text is [...] ious plagiarism checke[...] ubirdie.com.

Photo [...] o promote your work, [...] as been proven that us[...] e in getting the attenti[...] one.

Facebook photo ads are simple and straightforward. With the right image and accompanying text copy, people are much more likely to notice your brand. Photos are also excellent for increasing your audience's awareness of your products and/or services. People are much more likely to buy a product if they can see it first.

Consider using photo ads for any new products that your business is promoting. Photo ads are also very easy to make. You can simply add a photo to a page post, giving that post an automatic little boost. Photo ads work great for both desktop and mobile devices. As always, make sure the images you are using are either free of copyright or that you own the copyright or copyright release to them.

Video Ads: Facebook understands that people want different kinds of videos in different situations. For instance, if someone is on their mobile device, they are probably on-the-go and would prefer to watch something short. Meanwhile, if a person is on a larger device (like a laptop) and sitting on the couch, then they are likely more willing to watching a longer video.

For shorter videos, you might want to consider using in-feed ads. Whether your goal is to reinforce your brand or promote a new product, in-feed ads capitalize on quick, short spurts of attention from your target audience to promote your business.

Create a captivating video which quickly tells your story, and people, while scrolling through their feed, will stop to hear what your company has to say. Using video ads is a great way to drive sales. Furthermore, by combining video ads with product images and carousels, you can stimulate the interest of your audience and potentially increase your sales.

You can also create video ads that appear "in-stream," meaning the ad is shown after the viewer has begun watching a video. In-stream video ads can be as long as fifteen seconds, but the shorter they are, the better. Research shows that 70% of in-stream ads are watched to completion, with the audio/sound on. This allows you to deliver a more dynamic message to your audience.

Another advantage to using video ads on Facebook is that it allows your company to reach people that you might not otherwise reach with more expensive television ads. Research shows that Facebook video ads reach 37% percent more people in the age group of 18 to 24. Facebook is also creating new ways of using video to engage your audience. With Facebook 360 your customers can interact with the video to explore a 3D or panoramic environment. This is particularly useful for businesses like Real Estate Agencies - instead of posting a picture of a house, they can create a 3D or panoramic video of the interior of the house. This is much more eye-catching and attention-getting than a simple picture!

Finally, using Facebook Creative Hub, you can create "mock-up" or tester video ads, and then test them in real time. This allows you to see how various types of video ads may affect your audience and allows you to view these video ads from the perspective of your audience. This is especially important if you are interested in running a video ad in the News Feed of mobile phones, as the Mobile-view can restrict what appears on the screen. As always, make sure the images you are using are either free of copyright or that you own the copyright or copyright release to them.

Messenger Ads: Messenger ads are ads that appear in Facebook Messenger, as opposed to the News Feed of your audience members. Research shows that 2 billion Facebook messages pass between people and businesses each month. Using Messenger in this way is an incredibly effective way to engage current customers and to attract a wealth of new customers.

The best way to use Facebook Messenger, and to capitalize on its worldwide reach, is to place your ads on the Facebook Messenger home screen. This way, ads are mixed in with your customer list of conversations and are therefore difficult to ignore.

Messenger ads work in the same way that other ads do across the Facebook platform. Ads appear where they are most likely to boost your campaign, at the lowest possible cost to you.

When your customers tap on the ads appearing on their home screen, they will automatically and immediately be sent to whichever destination you selected during the creation of the ad, such as your website, your app, the product page you created, or a dialogue with your company on Facebook Messenger.

Using Facebook Messenger to promote your business has three essential advantages:

- You can start new conversations by using Facebook Messenger ads, which allows you to open a direct dialogue between your business or brand and the potential new or repeat customer.
- You can stay on top of Facebook Messenger conversations with existing or return customers by utilizing Facebook Messengers high-level view of existing or open conversations.
- You can re-initiate old conversations with customers that you have not interacted with or touched base with after a certain period of time.'

Below are the steps to take to create messenger ads.

1. Click create ads.
2. Choose messages objective.
3. Click the ad type messenger and select Sponsored message.
4. Chose which Facebook page top run the ad through.
5. After clicking the sponsored message, you can then have a custom audience based on your Facebook fan page messenger activity.
6. On placement level select automatic placement.

7. Click turn on when the messenger placement notification displays.
8. Choose your budget and schedule.
9. Click continue.
10. Choose image and text or text only.
11. Under page and links chose the page you want.
12. Select call to action, i.e. Learn more, sign up now, or contact us.
13. Click review order to check for errors.
14. Place order.

Each one of these steps is super easy. There are a few tips that can be used to make these advertisements more profitable.

- Tip 1: Only one message can be delivered to each person, within one ad set. In order to have more than one, you need to click Create Multiple New Ad Sets.
- Tip 2: By clicking show advanced options you can add additional targeting options. However, your audience size must have 20 or more people.
- Tip 3: In your edit placements section, you are only going to be able to select sponsored messages.
- Tip 4: The majority of your sponsored messenger ads will deliver in 3-5 days. If you want them to be delivered within specific times, then schedule them out for a week.
- Tip 5: There is a minimum bid that you can use. It will load in the bid strategy section for ad creation flow. In the US they recommend a bid of $30 per 1000 impressions.
- Tip 6: Schedule the ads to Run all the time. Sponsored ads do not support Ad scheduling.
- Tip 7: Optimization is set by impressions, the rate for sponsored messages is $30 per 1000 impressions.

Carousel Ads: Carousel ads allow you to use multiple images within a single ad. Each image can have its own link, and you can also use videos. Carousel ads allow you to showcase multiple products, various aspects of a single product or service, current promotions, or even convey a story about your company or brand that unfolds across each carousel card.

This ad format is dynamic and can be used to reach any number of your company's marketing goals. Carousel ads have a number of advantages over other types. Carousel ads give marketers a lot more space to be creative and engaging within the ten carousel cards available. They are also highly-interactive, allowing you to link to multiple websites or product pages. Your audience can also swipe or click on your carousel cards to move the story along, or visit whatever page you have linked to the image or video in question. And finally, because you have ten cards to fill with video or imagery, you have the flexibility to tell your story or feature your products in new and creative ways.

Whether you are showcasing multiple products, highlighting the various features of a single product, telling a story, or explaining a process, Carousel ads are a flexible and dynamic way to promote your business or brand.

Slideshow Ads: A Slideshow ad is like a video ad. It uses images, motion, text, and sound - all to tell a compelling or dynamic story. Slideshow ads work on any device and typically are not limited by slow internet or data speeds, the way some video ads are.

You can create a slideshow ad easily and quickly, whether for desktop or mobile devices, and you can use that slideshow to tell the story of your company, describe your product, or showcase a new line of products. You can use stock images made available by Facebook in the ad creation process, or even use existing video footage.

Slideshows are captivating, much like video ads are, but they are easier to create, less expensive to run, and less time consuming to maintain. They also tend to run more easily and more smoothly across all devices - from desktop to mobile, and everything in between. As always, make sure the images you are using are either free of copyright or that you own the copyright or copyright release to them.

Consider using a Slideshow Ad to determine what your audience may find compelling as a Video Ad. Slideshow Ads can be valuable "test runs" before you spend your time or money to create a Video Ad that may not generate the attention you had hoped for or planned on. Slideshow Ads are fast and easy to create and require very little planning on your part.

Collection Ads: Using a combination of video and imagery, Facebook Collection Ads are a great way to sell products, particularly via mobile phone. Because people are spending so much more time on their phones, and because this is changing the way they search, learn, and buy, Collections Ads are an ideal way to adapt to these changing circumstances. Your customers expect fast-loading, engaging, smooth video mobile experiences, so once a customer has tapped your ad, they can learn more about the features of your products seamlessly.

This ad format is seamless, and almost guaranteed to generate new business. Many Collections Ads include a video at the top of the ad, with a slideshow of images beneath the video - all of which are clickable and can provide your audience with direct access to your website, your product pages, and more. These ads are ideal for mobile devices because they tend to take up the entire screen of the mobile device - guaranteeing that the audience member viewing the ad is not distracted by any other content within their Facebook feed. You have their complete and undivided attention until they scroll away from the ad. As always, make sure the images you are using are either free of copyright or that you own the copyright or copyright release to them.

To make sure your Collections Ad is full of strong, effective content, consider trying the different aspect of the ad individually first. Post a Slideshow Ad with the images and test how well your audience responds to that Slideshow before including it in your Collections Ad. Furthermore, run a Video Ad alone as a test, before including it in your Collection Ad. This will guarantee that your Collections Ad is as effective as possible and that it will generate the response you have been looking for.

Step five

Once your ad set has been published, it is very important to pay attention to ad performance. Some ads may perform better than others, and you will need to find out why one ad performs better than others, that way you can adjust your ad set (and future ad sets) accordingly.

Facebook Ads Manager allows you to turn a particular ad off if you need to. You can also cancel your ad campaign altogether. In addition, if the parameters you set for your campaign are not generating any results, Facebook Ads Manager may waive the expense of the campaign, or reimburse you if they have already collected payment.

The following list will help you to understand the significance of the various results you may find in the Facebook Ads Manager report generator.

- Brand Awareness: This provides an estimation as to the number of people who may remember your ads within a two day period. This result is significant if you have objectives such as Video Views, Engagement, Brand Awareness, and Post Engagement. The reason they chose to a two day period is simply that studies show that if you recall seeing an ad two days after you initially saw it, you are significantly more likely to recall the name of the product or business a week or even a month later.
- Reach vs. Impressions: Reach is the number of people who have seen your ad at least one time. Reach is different from Impressions in that Impressions include people who have seen your ad multiple times, whether because they seek it out repeatedly or because it appears in their News Feed repeatedly.
- Traffic: This provides the number of actions your ads have contributed to your mobile app, and therefore recorded as "app events." This also provides the number of clicks your ads have received on desktop and mobile devices, which allows you to track how many people have used your ad to access your website - or whatever other clickable content has been attached.
- Engagement: This provides the total number of actions your ads have stimulated. This includes Facebook page "Likes" from ad engagement, the number of people that marked themselves as "Interested" or "Going To" an event your company has organized and streaming reactions from live broadcasts. This information is vital when determining whether or not your ad campaign has been successful.

Keep in mind that Facebook Ads Manager only bills you once a month, and only bills you for what has been spent on your ad campaign. Therefore - if you set a lifetime budget of $500 for your ad campaign, but only $25 of that $500 is spent in the month of January, then Facebook Ads Manager will only collect the $25 spent in January. This type of pay-as-you-go billing is incredibly useful for small business and those with small advertising budgets. Billing can be set up on an auto-pay schedule, using any major card. The auto-pay schedule can be customized so that you can even choose the day of the month that your payment is automatically withdrawn from your bank account or charged to your selected credit card.

Tip: *It is better to turn off an ad or ad set as opposed to completely deleting them. Deleting an ad or ad set is irreversible. Turning an ad or ad set off is like hitting that pause button. This way you can turn them back on later, if necessary, and after you have adjusted whatever parameter was preventing your ad from performing well. You can also turn the ad set off if you suddenly find that you need to make an emergency change to your advertising budget.*

Chapter 6: Instagram 2019

Instagram currently has more than 400 million users to the site on a monthly basis with more than a fourth of these using the site every single day. With numbers like these, it was only a matter of time before advertisers started taking notice and now more money is being spent on marketing via Instagram than ever before. While getting in now isn't exactly getting in on the ground floor, if you want to make money online, this is still a very profitable and fairly open market. You aren't the only one with this idea, however, so what follows are a number of ways to set yourself apart when it comes to advertising on Instagram.

Set your focus: Regardless of what you want to do with your Instagram account in the long term, the first thing that you will need to focus on is building a following, the more followers the better. The higher the number of followers you can boast, the more likely it will be that advertisers will give you the time of day and the more money you can get from advertising. In general, before you can start monetizing your Instagram page you are going to want to be able to prove that you have at least 10,000 followers and a strong following of individuals who check in with your page on a regular basis without actually following you.

The best way to start building your followers is with the right type of details in your profile. Information about yourself and the type of content you typically post is a good place to start, but only that, the best Instagram influencers include far more. This means including relevant keywords along with commonly used hashtags as this will make it less likely that you are simply posting photos into the void. This means you are going to want to start by coming up with a niche of photos that you are interested in working with every day for a prolonged period of time. If you have a topic idea but can't see yourself sticking with it for six months or more then you are going to want to head back to the drawing board as Instagram success should be measured in the long term.

Keywords and hashtags: Once you have a potential niche in mind, the next thing that you will want to do is to scope out other Instagram pages in the same niche and look to see what keywords and hashtags they are using. Keep in mind which pages you visited as you will need them later as well. While you are going to want to use popular keywords and hashtags, you are not going to want to simply stuff every one of your photos with as many as you can think of. Careful curation is key to attracting niche followers while not showing up so often that potential followers consider you spam.

Post, post, post: Once you have the limits of your content set, the next thing you are going to want to do is to post multiple times per day, every day. You will want to get on a schedule of posting and stick with it for long enough that people get used to checking back in with you at the same time each day. Once they are in the habit of checking in with you it is much more likely that they will follow you instead of having to track you down manually each time. It goes without saying that this will only work if you are taking high-quality pictures that people are actually interested in, if you aren't a photo-person then this online income stream probably isn't for you.

Take the right pictures: In order to determine the types of pictures that your future followers are interested in, head back to the pages you have already scouted out and determine which pictures are getting the most traction from followers. While copying pictures isn't going to get you anywhere, keeping these popular photos in mind when you take your own can give you some boundaries to your creativity that can be helpful to you in the long run. As you take pictures, focus on developing your own unique perspective as this is what followers are going to flock to your page to see.

Tag photos properly: Once you have pictures that you think potential followers will be interested in, it is important to go ahead and use the keywords and hashtags that you have come up with as often as possible. The more often various hashtags and keywords come up, the more likely your page will show up when those words are searched for. As your work expands, new keywords and hashtags are likely to become relevant, don't fight this and try and cram unrelated words where they don't belong, embrace the expansion as a way of gathering even more followers.

Join the community: When you are spending time on other influencer's pages, it is important to do more than luck, you are going to want to join the conversation. You are going to want to do more than simply like pages or include brief comments, the more you can prove you have something useful to say, the more likely that person's followers will check out your page as well. This means you are going to want to leave insightful feedback and start real conversations about topics that the niche is interested in. The more discussions you can start and participate in the better. These conversations shouldn't be thinly veiled adds for your own page either, focus on the quality of the content you are producing and people will track you down.

Tips for profile success

Choose the right handle: Your Instagram handle needs to be clear, simple, and easy to identify. You want to avoid using numbers or special characters in your profile handle because this will result in you being too challenging to find. The best handle you should use is just your business name, just like Nike (@nike), Walmart (@walmart), YumBakery (@yumbakery), TasteMade (@tastemade), NoRootsBoots (@norootsboots), and Target (@target) have. Using your business name is simple, easy to identify, and really starts building up brand awareness around your business so that people are more likely to recognize you in the future.

If your brand name is your name, you can simply use your name. However, this may not be ideal if your name is long, difficult to spell, or used by someone else already. In this case, you may want to shorten it to your first and middle name only or nickname like Jenni Farley of Jersey Shore did (@jwoww). Alternatively, if it is relevant to your business you may be able to add a simple prefix or suffix like Amanda Frances, a popular self-help personality, has done with her account (@xoamandafrances). Other examples of self-titled Instagram accounts that perform well and support in growing brand recognition include the ones held by Kim Kardashian (@kimkardashian), Oprah (@oprah), Deepak Chopra (@deepakchopra), Jess C Lively (@jessclively), or Will Smith (@willsmith).

The only time in which a special character may be deemed acceptable is if you use a period, which some companies have used. However, this can become very confusing for your followers as they may find themselves going to the original profile that has no special characters, rather than finding yours. For that reason, you should completely avoid adding special characters, strange spelling, or other unique elements to your handle. The more simple it is, the better it will be as it will make it much easier for your followers to find you online.

Take care with your bio: The most valuable real estate of your profile is your bio. On Instagram, you get about 200 characters, which can run out pretty quickly, meaning that you really need to spend time crafting the perfect one. Every word counts, and your bio should reflect exactly who you are as a company.

It really doesn't take that long of a time for you to go through and properly optimize the profile that you are using on Instagram, but it can definitely make a big difference on how many people will actually click on your site. It can also make a difference in how they view your brand. Some of the tips that you can follow to help optimize your profile include:

- In your bio, you should try to include the following information:
- Who you are
- What services you should provide
- Why should you follow them
- A link to your website for more information. You could even consider setting up a landing page that is specific for your visitors from Instagram, or you can make changes to the link to help promote a current campaign or other content.
- Make sure that the description and the images on your profile go well with the vibe that you want to see in your company.

- Use the logo for the company somewhere in the profile. This lets your users know that this profile is the official one for your company.
- Consider adding at least one brand specific hash tag to your profile. This makes it easier for your customers to know the profile belongs to you.
- If you are a local business or have your own store, consider including your physical location into the profile as well.
- Make sure that if you have other social media profile that your images, and any other content, stay consistent throughout.

Posting tips

Post at the right time: On Instagram, your audience will have a tendency to hangout on the platform at different times throughout the day, and throughout the week. Learning how to track your best posting times and post within these peak hours will ensure that your photographs get maximum engagement so that you can begin growing your account rapidly. With Instagram, the algorithm favors posts that are being interacted with quickly and genuinely, so the more likes and comments that you can accumulate early on, the better.

You can track the right posting times for yourself and your audience through Instagram's business analytics or through third party applications like PLANN or Iconosquare which both have intelligent and highly accurate schedules for you to plan your posts with. These platforms track your engagement and let you know when your profile tends to get the most views, likes, and comments through your new posts. Although third party apps will cost money to gain access to this information, it can help you rapidly grow your platform through having access to the right information to help you do so.

Post the right content: The trend on Instagram used to be to load your page up with selfies and have people liking your images, and while this behavior is still perfectly okay for simple sharing accounts, they are not ideal for brands or businesses who are looking to grow their platform in 2019. While selfies can (and should) be used to grow your page, you should refrain from having every post, or even every other post featuring you in a selfie. Instead, use selfies sparingly and place an emphasis on uploading other photos of interest to help you increase your reach in 2019.

If you do love sharing selfies and they do in some way relate to your brand, consider using your selfies more consistently in your story feed and less frequently in your actual newsfeed. This way, you can still share on-brand selfie images that can help you increase traction, but they do not dominate your feed and make you appear unprofessional or juvenile on the platform. These days, people prefer to see more thoughtful images that look similar to those that would be taken by professional photographers.

Be consistent: Having a consistent editing style will help you create some cohesivity in your feed. This makes sure that colors that are present in your photos generally look the same in every photo. Using apps like VSCO allows you to create presets so that you can use to utilize the same filter, temperature setting, contrast, highlights, etc. in every photo. This can be helpful, but it may be better to stick to editing each photo on an individual basis. This allows you to tweak different small aspects that benefit that specific photo. You can also use the filters in the Instagram app.

Photos with one of a few specific filters tend to get higher engagement than others, so using these may increase the favorability of your posts. Clarendon, Gingham, and Juno are the 3 most popular filters, followed by Lark and Mayfair. Using these filters, or similar filters from other apps, can increase engagement on your photos. You can also incorporate a specific personal touch that you add to each of your photos. Some people like to post photos with an element of darkness or shadows.

Doing this consistently can draw an audience that looks forward to seeing how you incorporate this element. It can narrow down the photos you are able to post, but it will help grow your following. Having one color that is present in each photo (for instance, a red shirt in one photo, a red building awning in the background of another, and a red coffee mug on a table in yet another) can be enough of an element of consistency.

Have the right captions: How you caption your photos can also be important. The caption should be relevant to the photo in some way, and it should add to the feel of the photo, not take away from it. Really long captions are a bit iffy in how they can read to your audience. An unnecessarily long-winded caption can detract from the beauty of your photo, and can cause your followers to not hit the like button because they get distracted reading the caption and scroll on.

A long caption that educates your followers on a topic within your brand can be a positive addition to your posts as it gives your followers something useful. This creates a value exchange.

Utilizing Instagram stories: Instagram stories are a powerful tool that can be used to not only nurture your existing following but also attract new followers into your business. When you use your Instagram stories correctly, you can create a significant influx of engagement from your followers, add a personal opportunity to connect with your brand and create a more interactive page overall.

On Instagram, people love interacting with the brands that they love and consuming as much of their content as they can, and Instagram offers plenty of ways for followers to do just that. As you upload to stories throughout the day, you create the opportunity for your followers to feel like you are genuinely thinking about them throughout the day, which establishes a connection of care and compassion between you and your followers. Not only will this help you maintain your existing followers, but it will also help new or potential followers see how interactive and intimate you are with your following, which leads to them wanting to be a part of your following as well!

The reason why stories works is simple, people are nosy and they like to know insider's information. This is not a bad thing, either, but rather just a simple human experience where we all desire to be a part of something bigger than ourselves and we want to connect with those around us to become a part of that "something bigger." You can position yourself as the facilitator of that "something bigger" by turning your brand into an experience that people can enjoy, and an entity that they can share an intimate and compassionate relationship with.

Stories give you a great option to do that because every picture or short clip you share reflects a part of your personal behind-the-scenes experiences. You can also curate your story feed to offer an even more exclusive and intimate feel by purposefully sharing things that will allow others to feel like they are genuinely connected with you through your feed.

Maximizing hashtags

Hashtags. You see them on practically every image that is uploaded on Instagram. Why do hashtags matter in these images and videos that get uploaded to the newsfeed? Because with a staggering number of images that get posted online daily by the millions of users around the world, delivering the right type of content to the right kind of people is difficult. Enter hashtags, the key to helping your content get viewed by the users who will be the ones keen on seeing it the most.

Want to maximize the potential of your posts being discovered across Instagram? Here are a couple of strategies to keep up your sleeve:

Use your hashtags strategically: Before every post is sent out, ask yourself how many hashtags do you think would be best? And which of these hashtags is going to benefit your ad the most? Having a quick think about these questions will save you a lot of time and prevent you from blindly hashtagging every word which you may *think* is going to help your post. Go with popular hashtags, but not the ones which are *too popular* where you run the risk of being lost in the tsunami of other content. 65,000 Instagram posts were analyzed by TrackMaven, and it was discovered that if you want your post to receive the highest possible engagement rate, then having 9 hashtags was the way to go.

Researching your hashtags: A simple, yet effective method is to simply do a quick search by typing in a few keywords on Instagram's search function. Then make a note of all the hashtags which get auto generated. It is also a great way to check up on the kind of hashtags your competitors are using. What sort of hashtags are your competitors or followers using at the moment? What are your influencers using?

Organizing your hashtags: Keeping your hashtags in an organized system is the best way to keep track of which ones you're using, how often you're using them and which ones have proven to get the highest number of engagement and traffic. You could either keep track of them using your own organizing system, keep them on an Excel sheet, or simply use Instagram's analytics tool to help you out.

Use the right hashtags
#Hashtags for Fitness in 2019:

- #fitinspiration
- #trainharder
- #fitfluential
- #running
- #yoga
- #fitness
- #winning
- #fitnessgoals
- #healthy
- #dedication
- #gymspiration
- #sports
- #gym
- #instarunners
- #workout
- #fitnesstips
- #fitfam

- #loveit
- #fitstagram
- #health
- #strong
- #training

#Hashtags for Fashion in 2019

- #modeling
- #fashionshow
- #instashoes
- #instahair
- #fashionista
- #trendy
- #luxurylife
- #cute
- #fashionable
- #instamakeup
- #fashionweek2019
- #photooftheday
- #model
- #instafashion
- #outfitoftheday
- #look
- #london
- #style
- #fashionblogger
- #fashiondesigner
- #fashionweek
- #design
- #instagood

#Hashtags for Food in 2019

- #instafood
- #yum
- #delicious
- #healthymeals
- #foodporn
- #nomnomnom
- #foodgasm
- #food
- #brunch
- #yummy
- #recipes
- #healthyeating
- #cooking
- #lunch
- #foodphotography
- #newrecipe
- #cookbook2019
- #healthyfood
- #breakfast
- #chef
- #healthycooking
- #wineanddine
- #healthy
- #diningout

#Hashtags for Travel in 2019

- #workfromanywhere
- #travel
- #summer2019
- #goexplore

- #digitalnomad
- #vacation2019
- #vacationtime
- #wanderlust
- #adventure
- #locationindependent
- #hiking
- #explore2019
- #travelpreneur
- #travelmore
- #adventuretime
- #roamtheplanet
- #workandtravel
- #travelblogger
- #travelblog
- #adventurelife
- #wonderfulplaces
- #traveller
- #doyoutravel
- #lovetotravel
- #adventureseeker

#Hashtags for Dog/pets in 2019

- #adorable
- #dog
- #cute
- #puppy
- #mypets
- #cutenessoverload
- #dogsofinstagram
- #puppylove

- #puppiesofinstagram
- #doglover
- #instapuppies
- #newpuppy2019
- #adventuredog
- #hikingwithdogs
- #dogsarethebest
- #puppylife
- #dogsarefamily
- #petstagram
- #puppypalace
- #lifewithdogs
- #pet
- #dogtraining
- #inspiredbypets
- #bestdog
- #weeklyfluff
- #instadog

These may be specific to the niche that they fall under but there are also ones that are generalized hot #hashtags that need to be considered for your Instagram profile. These are projected to catapult your engagement and Instagram audience to the top. #Hashtags for Instagram in 2019

- #fashionweek2019
- #newyear2019
- #newyears2019
- #musician
- #birthday
- #wedding
- #instalove
- #instafollow

- #followme
- #fun
- #happy
- #bestoftheday
- #workout
- #instagramhub
- #beautiful
- #smile
- #2019
- #aladdin2019
- #IT
- #cleaneating
- #red
- #love
- #tbt
- #iphonesia
- #igers
- #igdaily
- #blackandwhite,
- #stories
- #tweetgram
- #fitness
- #fit
- #instacool
- #musically
- #joker2019
- #instasize
- #photooftheday
- #nofilter
- #adventure
- #webstagram
- #picoftheday
- #repost

- #foodie
- #ootd (Outfit of the Day)
- #my
- #followback
- #likeforlike
- #instastyle
- #instamood
- #instalike
- #instagood
- #digitalnomad
- #travel2019
- #life
- #funny
- #travel

Now that you have your own cheat sheet for Instagram #hashtags it is time to start utilizing these to your advantage in 2019. Since a post on Instagram that contains a #hashtag get on average a 12.6% increase in engagement, it is a no brainer that you should use them in all your posts. #Hashtags help you reach a wider range of people that fall into that niche and will be interested in seeing your posts and reading what you have to say.

- #motivation
- #love
- #tbt
- #instagood
- #cute
- #Food
- #instamood
- #photooftheday
- #me
- #iphonesia

Try out a contest: Another thing that you may want to try out is running a contest. If you have a product that you can give away or something that you are willing to give away to help grow your business, then it may be a good idea for you to run a contest. There has to be a catch though. For example, for someone to have a chance of winning the contest, users need to repost a specific image and then tag you in the caption. Or you can invite your followers to use a special hashtag that you design and then use it on their own images.

If you feel like really expanding this out and getting other Instagram names on board, you can consider doing a giveaway. You can get on board with a few other profiles and influencers, and then everyone can be a part of this. This helps to give each profile or business a chance to reach new customers and can be a great way to build up your business like never before.

Instagram marketing mistakes to avoid

Don't be overly promotional: If your feed is filled with promotional content, your followers will receive more of a spam atmosphere from your blog. If your followers feel that they are disconnected from your blog, they may stop working with your posts. Some of your followers will eventually unfold. Make a balance between promoting your blog and engaging your followers actively.

Don't ignore the response/feedback you receive from your followers: You should actively seek your followers ' feedback. You can send them a questionnaire or talk to them to see what they really think about your blog. The response you receive from them could help you to work in areas in which you do not perform well in and can work to capitalize on areas in which you do well in.

Do not neglect captions: Try to prevent uploading images without subtitles. Subtitles help your followers gain more insight into the uploaded image. Captions are also what you use to communicate with your followers. The right types of headings give your followers the context of your posts and they can also contribute to your audience's response. Try not to go too far. 200 characters should be sufficient enough to pass on a message. Use emoji's as well, they can catch the eye of the viewer.

Don't neglect your community: Some people tend to think that their Instagram is just one way. They ignore the comments and messages of their followers. This never plays well. Your followers will feel that you are not interested in what they have to say, and they will flee. They may not even pay attention to your blog at all. Never wait for your followers to reach you, perhaps try reaching out to them!

Try not to underutilize the application: Use the Instagram stories, hashtags and inboxes to communicate with your followers and colleagues. Don't just take pictures, try attaching a link to your profile and explore the features. Instagram recently introduced a feature that allows you to upload multiple photos as a single post, try to make use of that. The more features you use; the more content you create.

Chapter 7: Paid Instagram Marketing

Paid advertising on Instagram is done the same way as it is on Facebook which means a majority of the information in chapter 5 is relevant here as well. In fact, if you start with Facebook before moving on to Instagram then all of your relevant choices will carry over. Overall, there are five different ways to create paid campaigns on Instagram including:

- You can create an ad in the Instagram app
- Through Facebook Ads Manager
- Using Facebook Power Editor
- Using Facebook's Marketing API
- Using Instagram Partners

Setting Up the Ad Placement

When you reach the stage of the set up for your ad campaign, there are quite a few options to choose from:

- The Facebook News Feeds – desktop and mobile
- The Facebook Right-Hand Column advertising
- Instagram
- In-Stream Video
- Instant Articles
- The Audience Network

For your first ad placement, you'll choose Instagram to get a new campaign on Instagram. However, you can choose numerous ad placements and use Instagram as one of the several options. It's possible to link several ad placements on Facebook allowing for your ads to appear in several newsfeeds and apps.

Ad specifications

There is more than one ad type to use when advertising on Instagram and the option is yours to choose which one best suits the ad you want to develop and post. Currently, there are a variety of different types of ads that can be used to market your ad, each one that would be perfect for a somewhat different marketing campaign. However, Facebook has more ad types than Instagram. It is extremely important to be aware of the different ad designs, so you'll be able to be knowledgeable in using them. Getting the highest ROI from Instagram marketing is what you want to strive for.

The questions that you'll want to be answered are:

- What are the different ad types on Instagram?

- What do you need to know to set up each individual ad type?

- What are the different ad specs on Instagram?

- What are the correct sizes for ads on Instagram?

- What examples of ads are the best to use on Instagram?

- Using specific types of ads – When should you use them and how to use them

Instagram gives you four different types of formats to choose from - carousel ads, single ad images, stories ads and video ads. The single image ads are the most straightforward, simple type of ads there is. Straight to the point, clear, concise, and they work brilliantly for ads which only want to feature single products or something with high visual appeal. You can't go wrong with this ad option.

Carousel ads are also known as multiple ad images. If you're planning to showcase several different products, it gives you more space to elaborate your content and the point that you're trying to make with your audience. Videos can also be slipped into your carousel ad selection to "spice things up" a little and create even more engaging content.

Video ads on Instagram work similar to Facebook, whereby they run on auto-play. They also start automatically playing without sound, although this is easily fixed by adding closed captions into your videos. The best video ads are kept at 60 seconds or less, and a minimum of 15 seconds at least to start.

Boosting your Instagram posts

Instagram's Ad system can be intimidating, especially when you're just started out and trying to figure out how things work. If you're looking to promote one of your posts quickly while still not entirely sure you're confident enough in your Instagram ad abilities, there's one option you could use to save the day - Boost Posts. With this option, you will only be paying to promote one specific post (so make it your best one!). As long as you have an established business profile on the social media platform, you can boost any post you have on your Instagram.

In your Instagram business profile, simply by clicking on a selected post, you will be able to see the option "Promote", which should be placed directly below the image. Clicking on this option will prompt you to select your focus objective, and you will only have two options to choose from. The first option could be to increase your website and profile visits, and the second option is to reach your target audience based on their location.

Influencer branding

One of the practices you can use for getting your brand out there and getting located is through using influencer marketing campaigns. Influencer marketing essentially means that you want to put your products into the hands of influencers and have them marketing your content, too. By having influencers sharing your products and brand with their own followers, you gain the opportunity to have your name put directly in front of their audience, too. As long as you are selecting the right influencers, their audience and your audience should be overlapping, meaning that they will help you gain access to your target audience much faster. With an influencer's seal of approval, you are far more likely to increase the effectiveness of your Instagram strategies and earn sales through your profile.

Launching an influencer marketing campaign first requires you to locate influencers who are likely to have the same target audience as you. Then, you want to consider how many followers they have and how active their following is. Influencers with more than 5,000 followers and with at least a 4% engagement rate should be considered effective early on. As you grow, you will want to continue looking for larger influencers who will be able to offer your brand even more exposure.

Influencer campaigns are costly in that you do have to offer free or discounted products to the influencers in order for them to have something to test, review, and promote to their audience. You will need to allot a budget towards this campaign that will account for the profit loss you will endure by giving away products or offering heavy discounts. However, as long as you are choosing the right influencer, this should all come back to you through their promotional activities.

Once you find influencers who appear to reflect your brand values and image and who have a similar target audience as you do, all you need to do is approach them. Typically, a well-put message that explains your intention and invites them to join your influencing opportunity is plenty enough to inspire an influencer to take you up on your opportunity. From there, you simply have to decide how much you want to give them, what you will compensate them with for their time and services, and what incentive you will provide their followers with to encourage them to purchase.

Tips for success

Keep it organic: The most effective Instagram marketing strategies are those that don't feel like they are actively trying to sell anything. Instead, if you are subtle about your branding then you will find that it is far more effective in the long run. Just because you are spending money on your Instagram ads does not make it acceptable to use pictures that feature a large logo or subpar images.

Additionally, it is important to never let your text take up more than 20 percent of any ad. If you try and fudge this rule then not only will your ads look cramped, they will get rejected as this is a firm policy for both Instagram and Facebook. When creating an ad you can use the provided grid tool to determine if a specific photo aligns with the current policy. Rather than using a text overlay you will find much more success by sharing the photo by itself and including any text in the caption.

When it comes to making your ad look organic, you are going to want to stick with pictures that have natural lighting and authentic looking pictures that are high quality. When it comes to showing off your brand's personality, you will also want to do so with the content and look of the picture, not by sticking a huge logo on all of your images. You should work hard early on to find the right mix of branded elements in your pictures to ensure that people who see it will associate it with your brand, without beating them over the head with the purpose of the picture.

Additionally, it is important to keep in mind that if you have too many focal points in your image then it becomes difficult for the viewer to decide what to focus on. Instead, you are going to want to stick to a handful of focal points, including a single branded element, and avoid borders or complicated filters completely.

When it comes to image quality, it is important that you only post high-resolution pictures that are clean and detailed. You should also strive to use images that relate to your niche and things that your audience can apply to their real lives as doing so will immediately improve your clickthrough rating. It is also important to keep in mind that consumers tend to trust user generated content compared to brand created content practically two to one which means that determining a good way to include this type of content in your advertising is almost guaranteed to generate a positive response.

It is also important to avoid resting on your laurels when it comes to the types of ads you create as your audience is always interested in something new and they tire of advertising quicker than anything else. One good way to split the difference between starting from scratch every time and keeping things fresh is to consider telling a variety of stories around a central theme. This way you will have some general guidelines that will keep you from having to reinvent the wheel with each new ad, and viewers will continue to see new things on a regular basis.

Look for opportunities for sponsored posts or paid shout-outs: When it comes to spending money on Instagram, one of the best ROIs is to find well-known names in your niche and then reach out to them about paid shout-outs or sponsored posts. This strategy worked for *Foundr* magazine which was able to pick up 500,000 Instagram followers in its first six months, 10,000 of which were accrued in the first two weeks of operation thanks to proper use of this strategy.

While you should certainly be willing to go the pay to play route when you are reaching out to relevant individuals you will want to start by offering a share for share with larger accounts. This is where two users share the other's content on their Instagram. While this is theoretically useful, the people you should be reaching out to will be significantly more influential in the space, which is why you will need to be willing to pay when necessary. If this is the case, then you may not need to pay for a full share, you could instead get a simple shout out for less money which is often nearly as effective as it make's that influencer's followers curious to learn more about you.

To get started with this type of approach you can look for shout-out groups related to your niche which often contain other Instagram marketers who can point you in the right direction. Using this approach is how Foundr was able to use a variety of shout-outs that cost about $100 each, by asking that the influencers include a call to action regarding checking out the new content. The results also work on a larger scale, if you have the funds to pull it off. In fact, one study estimated that paying those with more than a million followers to keep content in their feed for approximately three hours generates $5 worth of exposure for every $1 spent.

When it comes to reaching out to specific influencers the best place to start is with their bio. If, when reading their bio, you find an email address, then the odds are high that they accept sponsored branding placements.

Don't underestimate email: While having a large Instagram following is sure to make spreading brand awareness easier than it would otherwise be, if you are looking to generate serious business results then you are going to want to work to get your followers subscribed to an email newsletter. This is more difficult on Instagram than with some other social media platforms as Instagram does not natively allow for any live links in comments or captions.

Where you can place links, however, is in your bio link. This link needs to be short, memorable, and simple. Luckily, creating this type of URL is easy with bit.ly or other, similar, sites that allow you to generate a short, fully custom, URL. Back to the previous example of *Foundr*, using this method they were able to generate 30,000 subscribers in their first month. For a reasonable fee, companies like MailChimp will automate a majority of the email newsletter process so that you can turn your Instagram into a true conversion machine.

Take better pictures: When it comes to finding the right pictures to use, the first thing you are going to want to avoid is using a picture that you don't own. With so many different photos floating around online, it can be easy to think that a given picture is in the public domain, this is rarely the case, however, so if you are unsure of where a specific picture came from, don't use it. There are few things that can do more harm to your online persona than being accused of thievery, do yourself a favor and ensure your pictures are coming from legitimate sources. Additionally, it is important to avoid stock photo sites as much as possible because if users see the same picture in multiple places then they are going to naturally assume the content is the same as well which means they are less likely to finish reading whatever you have created because the impression is that they have read it before.

When at all possible, you are going to want to generate the pictures that you use yourself. Not only will this encourage your readers to feel more engaged with you over time, but it will also help keep your content feeling fresh. Depending on the size of the pictures you plan to use, and the quality of your smartphone, you may not even need specialized equipment. If you do decide to make your own photos ensure that they remain both relevant and visually interesting in their composition. A boring picture is still better than nothing at all, but only just.

Don't forget IGTV: The IGTV platform, which is built directly in to the Instagram platform, can be found on your home page. IGTV is designed to allow you to take videos with your phone and then share them on your channel for as long as you desire so that your audience has more to watch. IGTV is a great way to increase your following, as these videos stay in-place for as long as you leave them up, meaning that followers can look back through your IGTV channel and watch stuff that you put up days, weeks, months, or even years ago once it has been around long enough.

You can leverage IGTV to create new followers by creating excellent IGTV videos and then promoting them elsewhere online so that people are more likely to click over to your channel and watch. Once they see your video and the quality of the content you create, they can choose to follow your page in order to get more if they decide that they like you.

The big key opportunity with IGTV is that you can promote your IGTV channel just like you would a YouTube channel or any other free video content. By creating great content and then sharing it around you can encourage individuals to go over to your Instagram in order to be able to actually see the video. This means that you can funnel people from Facebook, Twitter, Snapchat, e-mail, and any other social media platform that you may be on to Instagram so that they can catch your free content and learn from it.

In order to make your content popular, you are going to need to make sure that the IGTV videos you make are worthy of receiving views. In other words, you need to be creating high quality, interesting, and relevant content that your audience actually wants to pay attention to so that when you share it to other platforms they are more likely to click through to your channel and actually watch the content that you created. The best way to create valuable content is to offer entertainment, insight, or guidance in relation to your industry so that your audience is more likely to pay attention to it and watch it.

Chapter 8: YouTube 2019

These days, building a YouTube channel really has to be done right if you are going to out-compete everyone else who is trying to create the same type of success that you are seeking. That being said, if you approach your channel with the right intention, attention, and desire to create success, you can absolutely out-compete anyone else who may also be trying to access your target audience. You simply need to have a greater desire, more consistency, and the right tools in place to help you access your audience in ways that actually work.

Creating the perfect YouTube page

Putting together a YouTube channel is pretty simple to do. The website does a great job of walking you through it, and with a little exploring, you'll be a master.

About section: The About section is often overlooked and not given nearly as much attention as it should in most YouTube profiles. This is mostly because when you look at somebody's profile, it's hidden in another tab, rather than right at front, in contrast to the majority of other social media networks where it's right at the front.

While your character limit is not nearly as cramped as others, it should still be short, sweet, and simple. Treat it like you only have 100 characters, and only put the most important things in there. Say what you do, your message, and your goals. You don't have to use hashtags.

At the end of your description, don't forget to add in all the links to your other social media pages, and if you have a website too. YouTube allows up to 5 links, which should be plenty. You can even customize hyperlinks up to 30 characters. You should also consider putting your business email, in case there are people who want to collaborate with you.

Your cover and profile image: Keep both your profile image and your cover image simple. Your logo can act as your profile picture, and for your cover image, consider a large image with your slogan, or a small description of who you are. Keeping it simple, at least at first, is a good bet. Just make sure it's visually pleasing.

Your YouTube trailer: YouTube actually allows you to choose a video to put right front and center on your page. One idea is to put together a trailer, clips and things all put together to really show what your channel is about. For just starting out, just keep putting your best work up there. The absolute best video you've got, the one that best represents your company and your channel should be the first video your potential customers see.

Creating quality video content

Starter tips: The following tips will help you create awesome YouTube videos:
camp
- Use a lot of light: you want your video bright, not dark, thus light is necessary.
- Use a clear background: filming on dirty and chaotic backgrounds (unless it's intentional) would have the video come out low-quality and make you seem unprofessional.
- Clear audio: audio quality is as important as video quality. Actually, most people have more patience for a poor-quality video than bad audio.

- Avoid shaky footage: it makes it seem like the person filming was ill or you had used an extremely outdated device. If you shake too much, use a tripod.
- Work on your camera presence: looking fidgety, nervous and uncomfortable will distract the viewers. You want to come across as someone who knows what they are doing.

Uploading your video: Uploading a video to YouTube is really easy. Open up the YouTube main page and along the top, you will see an upwards pointing arrow. Click on this arrow to go to the upload page, where you can select the video file that you previously edited. Once the video is uploading you can customize the headline, thumbnail, description, and tags.

Later on, if you want to make more changes to your video then click on your icon in the top left corner of the YouTube main page. A drop down menu will display, and you will want to click Creator Studio. This is where you can find all the tools you need to manage your YouTube page. In the right hand sidebar you can find your "video manager", here you can go to individual videos to edit their captions, edit the video itself, or change any other information regarding your video.

The importance of frequency: On YouTube, one of the most important things that you can do for your growth is to consistently publish new content for your viewers. Many people forget that YouTube is a social media website, which means it favors accounts that are engaging in regular sharing back and forth. The more frequently you upload to your channel and have friends and viewers engaging with your videos, the more YouTube is going to favor your content and drive you up in the rankings when it comes to people searching for your content.

Think about any other video-based system where episodes are frequently shared, such as cable, the more consistently content is released, the more people are going to tune in and pay attention to that content. The pilot episode may get a lot of hits, and then, after that, it may dwindle down, but the consistent releasing of new episodes keeps people coming back and watching more. Eventually, the audience grows again as people come back to learn more about the growing story line and are captivated by the show. The same goes for your YouTube channel: you might get a lot of hits early on, but if you do not maintain your frequency the content that you do share is going to stop getting views. You need to maintain your momentum and continue growing it if you are going to generate continued success with YouTube, which means that you need to ensure that you are consistently uploading videos.

Another massive benefit of frequently uploading new content is that you are driving new traffic to your channel on a consistent basis, which means that not only will your new videos get visibility but you will also increase the visibility of older ones. As people land on your videos, they will hopefully take the next step and visit your channel to see what other videos you offer. Through that process, if you have plenty of high quality videos uploaded that are relevant to your niche, these individuals will click through to your older videos and watch them as well. The more they do this, the higher your older videos will rank and the better your overall channel will rank as well, which means that your growth rate will increase exponentially.

Create a consistent intro and outro: An important factor that you need to consider when it comes to creating your YouTube channel is the consistency of your video content. You can create consistency by keeping your core message and approach the same, but you can further amplify that consistency by having short intro and outro clips that help introduce and summarize your videos. This is like the theme song and intro that your favorite shows play, followed by a short credits scene at the end of every episode, which helps you recall all of your favorite shows effortlessly.

Chances are you can still remember the *Friends* theme song, even if you never really got into the show, simply because it was used so many times and it played on television for so long. This consistency is exactly what you can create in your own videos by creating short intro and outro clips with music and information that introduces your audience members to your channel.

A simple intro is all you need, but it is highly recommended to keep you consistent and easy to be identified in the online space. Make sure that the music you use is royalty free, or that you purchase the rights to it so that you are not going to face any copyright infringements from your clips. Then, simply choose some high quality images or a short high quality intro film that you are going to lay the music over. Add in some words that introduce the title of your channel and the episode, and maybe your usernames for other social media platforms and your website, and you're done!

Try to keep your intro to under 25 seconds to ensure that you are getting the consistency across without overdoing it. If your clips are too long, your audience may click to a "similar" video for the same information because it took too long for you to get to the point, which would completely miss the point of this branding feature!

Post your content on multiple networks and advertise properly: If you look at some of the most profitable YouTube stars you will see that they link to their social media profiles in their description of each video. This is a method of cross posting for more added engagement. This also is a way of getting organic self-promotion. By cross posting your links you can gain more engagement and followers and build a wider audience that is loyal to your brand. Once your videos are uploaded share them with the other social media pages that you have. You can also cross promote between your different YouTube channels. With the advantage of YouTube's advertising options, you are able to promote your content on other channels that are relevant and relatable.

Monetize: Once your new videos are regularly generating at least 1,000 views per video you will know that you have enough of a subscriber base to begin to successfully monetize your page outside of just your affiliate links. Luckily, the key to doing so is already built into your channel through what is known as the monetization tab. This tab can be found in the options menu and it will let YouTube start placing relevant advertisements before your videos. You will also want to connect your channel to Google AdSense which, in turn, will turn on various advertisements based on each viewer's browser history. More information on AdSense can be found at Google.com/AdSense.

Both of these types of advertisements will start out with a pay per click structure, though if you reach enough subscribers you will eventually gain access to pay per view advertisements as well. If you plan on making money in this fashion it is important to never use copyrighted material in your videos. A pay per click structure typically pays out 20 cents per click, with 1,000 views being enough to assume 10 people will actually click on the advertisement in question. If you gain enough of a following to qualify for pay per view type ads, then you can expect to make roughly $3 for every 1,000 views the ad receives.

Become a YouTube Partner: While this final step is crucial when it comes to maximizing this potential affiliate marketing revenue stream, it isn't something you can do by yourself. Instead, all you can do is continue posting quality content, and when your videos hit a high enough number of regular viewers you will receive a letter from. Once this occurs you will then be able to place affiliate links directly in your videos as opposed to just in your video descriptions. This means you are going to want to ensure you shorten your links appropriately as no one is going to want to click on a URL that takes up three lines of the video description all by itself.

Tools for increasing reach

Tools, apps, and software to ease things and increase reach

Building a YouTube channel takes a lot of work especially if you are trying to grow your business. Fortunately, there are some amazing tools that you can use to help you with your channel. These tools and apps will help you to manage your channel, increase your reach, and edit your videos. Here are some of the tools and apps that you can use to enhance your YouTube channel.

- Tube Buddy: Tube Buddy is considered the single most useful YouTube toolkit. It is an essential toolkit that you need to have if you are to be successful. It comes with more than 60 different features that help you with almost anything that you need. Tube Buddy will generally help you to promote your channel and videos, ensure that you are productive, and also aid with your YouTube SEO.

- Snappa: If your YouTube channel is to grow and increase your reach, then you need a tool that lets you create excellent artwork and images. Snappa is among the top tools out there for YouTube videos. It will enhance your videos and enable you to come with great visuals through its premade templates. It is advisable to always use high quality image editing and enhancing tools for your YouTube and Snappa is excellent even when compared to other tools in the market.

- Creator Studio App: If you have a number of apps and wish to promote your business through them, then you will need some assistance. This is where the Creator Studio app comes in handy. This is a powerful tool that lets you do just about everything on your YouTube channel except perhaps creating the original video. You also get to find out how your video is performing and receive metrics and lots of other things as well.

- Wix: You will need this app if you plan to monetize your YouTube account. As a small business owner, your aim of using social media sites like YouTube is to help you find customers in order to sell your products for a profit. For this to happen successfully, you will need a website.

Affiliate marketing

You will also want to sign up for one or more affiliate marketing programs, most likely starting with what is known as Amazon Associates. Once you are a member of the program you can then link to any page on Amazon.com and receive a percentage of the total sales price of any items that visitors from your site purchase. The specific amount you receive per item sold varies based on the number of visitors your blog regularly sees. Don't be afraid to shop around when it comes to affiliate programs as they can vary drastically in terms of payout.

Once you start working as an affiliate marketer, it is important to not go overboard on the sales pitch as this is a good way to start losing all those viewers you worked so hard to gain. Instead, it is a better idea to create videos as usual but once a week introduce a new segment where you review a particular product that you think your niche would care about. This way, your viewers are getting useful content and you get to profit from the reputation you have created for yourself.

Depending on the goals of your content marketing strategy, reviewing products related to your niche or sub-niche is often one of the best ways to bring in new members of your target audience. A review of a product will naturally slip past the standard defenses that many people put up towards sales pitches while still containing virtually all of the same information of a good pitch without any of the traditional stigma that typically comes along with the process. Remember, a review can help customers avoid wasting their money on a shoddy product while a sales page is considered an especially pushy advertisement.

When it comes to these types of product reviews, it is important to be as honest about a product's strengths and weaknesses as possible. Especially when you first start affiliate marketing, if you take on a product that is questionable without pointing out all of its flaws and justifying your recommendation then you are likely going to train readers not to listen to you when it comes to products.

Remember your YouTube page is part of your brand which means you need to protect it first and foremost, no matter what the commission per sale might be. You want your reviews to include anecdotes of you using the product in question, with pictures. Your readers should be able to easily put themselves in your shoes.

The pay-per-sale commission model can lead to big windfalls for vloggers, but only for those who choose the right products to sell. As an affiliate marketer, all you can do is convince your readers to click the link in question, it is then up to the seller to complete the sale otherwise you don't get anything. As such, when it comes to products that you wish to advertise, be sure to check out the seller's page and ensure that it is going to hold up its end of the bargain.

The easiest way to go about doing product reviews is to focus on a single product or group of products with an exceptionally critical eye. This means you are going to want to single out the various weaknesses of the product or product line as well as focusing on its strengths and what makes it unique. It is important to keep in mind that this type of content needs to come off as unbiased as possible otherwise the illusion will be ruined. This means it is important to intersperse positive reviews with negative ones to allow your target audience to come to the right conclusions about your review integrity. When writing these reviews feel free to include two or three links where the reader can purchase the product if they are so inclined.

Broad strokes reviews: Depending on the type of products that are relevant to your target audience, you may find an in-depth review of products to not only be difficult to film but relatively useless as well. Instead, you may want to focus on brief reviews that typically include just a brief shot of the product and a few hundred words outlining the product's bullet points before including an overall rating and links to purchase if relevant. These types of reviews are typically most effective with cheaper products which viewers just want a little information on before making their purchasing decisions.

As an added bonus, these types of reviews often generate a higher rate of link click-throughs as users are more likely to click the link in question with the goal of finding out more information on the product. These posts are often going to include a round-up of likeminded products in each post and a ranking of the same from best to worst. This is because of the fact that your target audience is going to be much more likely to watch 1 video outlining 10 products than 10 videos outlining one product each as the single video will frequently be perceived as a more effective use of time.

Comparisons: If a product that you have a vested interest in stands up particularly well when compared to other products in the same category then a comparison piece can be a great way to make that superiority known. All you need to do then is to compare the strengths and weaknesses of each along with any feature parity and let the stronger product speak for itself. If you are particular fond of a given product but don't want to come off sounding biased than a comparison video is a great way to go about doing it. The more types of products you include on this type of review the better, if you do it properly you can attract plenty of additional traffic simply because you are a good resource for those looking to make the right purchasing decision right now.

Negative slant reviews: Negative slant reviews are different than outright negative reviews as the goal of a review with a negative slant is to convince those who are naturally contrarian by nature by including caveats in the review that are sure to hook them and draw them in. As such, to create this type of content you are going to want to focus on the positive qualities of the product in question before going on to lament how it is too complex, too expensive and the like which makes it a product that is only the most suited for the most committed or most experiences, users in a given niche. When done properly, plenty of people will be willing to prove you wrong and will put their money on the line to do so.

Chapter 9: Paid YouTube Marketing

Creating a campaign

Creating a paid YouTube marketing campaign is quite similar to the process you would go through via Facebook or Instagram. The steps are outlined below.

Creating your campaign

Step 1: Log in to your YouTube channel.
Step 2: On YouTube Ads, click on Get Started with AdWords for video.
Step 3: Select your time zone and currency of choice.
Step 4: Name your campaign.
Step 5: Sign in to your AdWords account.
Step 6: Login to your YouTube account again.
Step 7: Enter your daily budget.
Step 8: Click the select video button.
Step 9: Search for your YouTube channel.
Step 10: Select the video that you want to advertise.
Step 11: Write your ad copy.
Step 12: Choose your thumbnail
Step 13: Enter your landing page and click save.
Step 14: Create a new target group.
Step 15: Choose your maximum cost per view.
Step 16: Enter your keywords.
Step 17: If you'd like to target an audience further, click Add YouTube Search Keywords and Add Targets button to put more keywords.
Step 18: Save and start your campaign.

YouTube-specific ad formats

There are also a variety of YouTube-specific formats you can use for your ads, as well as some interactive elements you can add to give things that extra punch.

TrueView In-Stream: This ad immediately immerses viewers in your content. The ad plays for five seconds and after that, users are given the option to skip the ad, though it will continue to play if they don't actively choose to skip it. This type of format is ideal if you want to play an ad for your brand prior to, after or during related video content.

TrueView Discovery: This ad appears next to related YouTube videos, on YouTube search results, or on the YouTube desktop and mobile homepage. This type of advertising doesn't have an upfront cost, though you can still set how much you would ultimately like to spend. You pay for each click that you receive from a viewer whenever they click through and begin to watch your video. This option is great for reaching new viewers during the point of discovery when they are already looking to watch something new.

Bumper Ads: This ad is six seconds or shorter and plays before, during, or after another video, but unlike previous options, it is not possible for viewers to skip the ad prior to its completion. The rate for this is calculated per 1,000 views your ad will receive. This option is great if you are looking to simply get the word out about your brand to as wide of an audience as possible. The best ads that take advantage of this format are those that are memorable for a specific reason with a clear message.

Interactive options: You can add interactive elements to your video ads to drive deeper engagement allowing you to select the options that best support your campaign goals.

- Call to action overlay: This overlay appears once the video begins and is controlled by the viewer. They can close the overlay, or click on it and be directed to a website or YouTube channel that is predetermined.

- Card: This options plays a brief two-second teaser and is available in a variety of options. For example, you can link to a video or video playlist on YouTube.

- End screen: This screen shows up for a few seconds after your video plays and can be expanded to allow the viewer to uncover additional information when they interact with it.

- Companion banner: Accompanies a TrueView In-Stream ad as a clickable thumbnail. It can guide viewers to take an action such as "Watch more" or "Subscribe."

Watch the analytics

The first thing you want to monitor when you go to your YouTube analytics is your overall retained viewership ratings because this is what YouTube cares about the most. If this number is high, chances are the rest of your analytics are going to be higher as well.

If this number is low, or if it is dropping, chances are something in your overall strategy is failing and you need to start searching through the rest of your analytics to get to the bottom of it and see what is going on. Through this search, you can see where your strategies are falling flat and what you need to do in order to improve your content, your rankings, and your overall growth.

When you read your analytics, make sure that you not only pay attention to your overall channel growth but to your video performance as well. The performance of each individual video is going to tell you whether or not your strategies are working in each video, especially as your channel continues growing. As your channel grows and these numbers have a longer history, you can start recognizing the trends on your channel to get a distinctive idea as to what your viewers like and what they do not like on your channel.

These trends will show you everything from what titles draw the most attention to what styles of videos keep your viewers watching the longest, and even what content gets the most views in general. You want to start producing more of the content that meets these three criteria: gets the highest views, with the highest retention ratings, and the best engagement ratings.

So, videos that have many people clicking through to watch it, that have people watching it all the way through, and that have people liking or commenting on or subscribing to your channel are the videos that you want to favor. You can create videos similar to these ones, with new subject matter of course, and using or improving the strategies that you used on those videos to further increase your success on YouTube and get even more followers.

Tips for success

While there is no perfect formula for creating a successful video ad, there are a variety of things you can aim for to ensure your money is as well spent as possible.

Focus on the story of your brand: While bumper ads are effective for distilling a branded message down to its essence, longer ads are great for getting viewers invested in your brand's personal narrative. With that being said, the first five seconds are all you are typically going to have to capture the viewer's interest which means you need to start with a bang if you want anyone to come along for the ride. If you are going to include interactive elements then this will be the time for that as well.

It is important to leverage your best content in this instance as well, which is why you would do well to show various versions of your ad to a test audience for feedback before you settle on the one that best reflects your core goals and gets your message across as persuasively as possible. You will also want to ensure that it ends with a clear course of action that the viewer can take to move forward and actively consume more of your content. It is also important to ensure that viewers have time to act by including an end screen that lasts between five and 10 seconds.

Set reasonable goals: Many new social media marketers make the mistake of trying to cram as much into their first paid advertisement as possible in hopes of ensuring they get the most out of their initial investment. This is a flawed strategy, however, as by trying to do everything at once, they end up accomplishing far less than may otherwise be the case. Instead, it is important to pick a single goal per ad as this way you will be far more likely to actually accomplish it.

Chapter 10: Twitter 2019

Twitter has an incredibly high conversion rate for people who are on the platform promoting their brands. As you will learn about in this chapter, Twitter is far from going anywhere any time soon, despite what many people are eager to claim every year for the past few years. What's more, it can actually serve as a powerful branding platform for companies who share a similar demographic as the one that hangs out most on Twitter.

The approach that you have to each social media site that you work with should be a bit difference. You won't be able to use the same strategy that you do with Twitter as you do with your Facebook marketing plan. It is important that you learn more about the way Twitter works and the best way to use it in order to get the best benefits.

There are many different ways that a business is able to utilize Twitter in order to reach their needs. Some of the main ways include:

- Managing their reputation
- Branding themselves
- Networking so they can find other similar businesses and potential customers in the industry
- Interacting with their customers, and potential customers.
- Driving engagement for some of the promotional activities that they are working on
- Sharing the content and information that they have about their business and about their products.

Just like with all of the other social media options discussed in the previous chapters, most of these activities are going to have to do with interactions. It is not just about broadcasting out your content, like what can happen with Instagram and Facebook. Twitter works because of open communication.

Build a Twitter strategy

The first step in creating a strong strategy is having the right profile to back you up. Since Twitter is known for having an average of up to 80% of people who land on your page click your link, it is important that your profile gives people a reason to click through and check out your website. You can do this by ensuring that your profile looks attractive and features all of the information that people need to know about your business right off the bat.

When you first sign up for your Twitter account, you will be guided to choose a profile picture. Aside from that, you will need to click into the editor link to change your cover image, update your username, create your description, and add your link into your bio. You can do this by going to your account and tapping "edit."

The first thing you will want to do is change your username, as Twitter will have yours set to an automatically generated one that likely makes no sense to you or your brand. On Twitter, your username can only be 15 characters long, so if your brand name is longer you are going to need to find a way to shorten it without making it confusing or hard to remember or spell.

Next, you want to update your description to include a simple introduction to what your brand is about and what you offer. This should be engaging and interesting so that people can immediately resonate with you and your image and decide whether or not they want to follow you or click through to the link that you will also provide. You can provide the link on the same page as where you have updated the bio on your page.

Know your target market: You need to be very clear on who the target market for your business is. And which target markets you're trying to pull into your circle. If you don't know who your customer base is, you can't create the right kind of content for them to keep them coming back. Ask yourself who they are and how your business can help them. Ask what your business has to offer that would draw these customers in. Once you've answered those questions, then look at the content you are posting on your social media platform. Is it relevant, useful, beneficial, and interesting enough for your target customer base? Is this what they are after? Will this help them? Is the content relevant to your business? Does it engage the customers enough to provoke a response or reaction from them?

Be effective with your hashtags: Just like Instagram, hashtags play a key role on Twitter in helping to drive traffic and spot what the latest trending topics or discussions are. Hashtags are an excellent way for audiences to notice your posts. But there's one difference to using hashtags here compared to Instagram – on Twitter, keep the hashtags to one or two at best. Twitter is not the platform for multiple hashtags. Because the hashtag usage is limited, just like the content you're posting, you need to carefully consider which hashtags to use. Opt for the ones that work best with your business, and ones that are relevant. Don't just dump a hashtag in there for the sake of having a hashtag. It loses all value and meaning then.

Schedule tweets intelligently: Being active on Twitter does not mean infesting the timeline of your followers with 10,000 messages a day, or posting ten content within an hour and "sleeping" for the rest of the day.

If you want to attract - but above all, keep - new followers you have to intelligently measure your tweets and distribute them throughout the day. To facilitate this task you could use services like Buffer, which allows you to schedule the publication of new posts on Twitter and Facebook in a simple and fast.

To subscribe to Buffer, connected to its homepage, click on the Sign in button and log in with your Twitter account. Then provide an email address and password to use to sign up for the service and create your first scheduled tweet. To do so, type the message to be posted on your account in the appropriate text field, presses the arrow next to the Add to queue button and select the Schedule post option from the menu that appears. Buffer is also available as an app for Android and iPhone, so you can program your tweets from the smartphone.

Taking the time to plan ahead of the holidays and any other special events that occur in your company can ensure that you have plenty of time. You can use this to pick out trending hash tags for your topics and create some high quality content without feeling rushed.

Instead of waiting until a few days before, you should make it your goal to come up with a campaign no later than two weeks before the scheduled time. There are also various calendars that you can find online that will help you look at the upcoming holidays so you can make a comprehensive plan of what you want to write your Tweet for.

Find the right people to follow: By following those that think exactly like you will help to increase your following and gain your brand a much better trust factor among your consumers. By following the ones that are gaining huge audiences you will be able to increase your reach through their re-follow. With Twitter, if you have followed someone and they like your content or re-follow you back there is an option to share the content that they like. This will spread the awareness of who you are and what your company is about. By following accounts that are not connected to famous people you will be able to get noticed for your follow and they, in turn, can share the favor and follow back.

Utilize the @mention often: On Twitter, there is an option for you to @mention others. This is a way to tag them in your posts. Anytime someone @mentions you, you should respond, however, do not only communicate with the ones that @mention you. You must communicate with others as well. It is best to find interesting topics that you are passionate about and then communicate with them about the topics that are hot topics. When you reply to topics that are hot topics you will be able to be seen by millions of other people that have been commenting on the post as well as those that will comment at a later date. This brings notice to your business.

You can also use the online target topics searching option to look for industry mentions and terms that would help you to find your subject matter. If you notice a Tweet that comes in which is relevant to your subject matter, then follow it and begin to communicate within the thread. You must be specific with the topics that you are looking for so that you can get a dedicated post that is about the topics which matter most to you. This will also allow you to interact with those potential consumers that genuinely care about your content.

Chapter 11: Paid Twitter Marketing

With millions and millions of tweets sent every single hour of every single day, it can be easy for the message of even brands that are well-known to get lost in the shuffle. If you are interested in using Twitter as a primary social media marketing platform then paying to make sure your ads get in front of the users who are most likely to actually use your product is a great way to ensure your message is heard above the cacophony that is Twitter at any given moment. Twitter ad engagements were up more than 50 percent in 2018 while costs were down making it a great time to look to Twitter to increase your social media marketing reach even further.

Twitter ad types

Promoted tweets: When you purchase a promoted tweet what you are essentially doing is paying to display a tweet to people who are not actively following you on Twitter. These tweets function just like any other and can be liked, tweeted, etc. Importantly, they also look like normal tweets with the exception that they have a small label that indicates they are promoted. Promoted tweets will be seen in individual user's timelines, at the top of relevant search results, and on user profiles and are visible on both the desktop and mobile version of Twitter.

Promoted accounts: Promoted accounts are a great way of reaching out to members of your niche who may not yet already be following you. Paying for a promoted account will allow your account to be seen in the timeline of potential followers, as well as in the suggestion field and at the top of search results. They are clearly identified as promoted, but they include a follow button as well.

Promoted trends: When a topic is trending on Twitter it is safe to assume that it is one of the most talked about topics online at the moment. Paying for a promoted trend makes it possible for you to move a specific hashtag to the top of the list. When a user clicks on your promotion they will then see a list of search results related to the topic, with your content at the top of the list. As more and more people get on board with the hashtag, your brand will gain additional exposure.

Twitter promote mode: While the rest of this chapter will outline how to set up a specific Twitter campaign, there is also an option for those who want to get started as quickly as possible. This mode costs a flat fee per month and, once activated, promotes the first 10 tweets you send out each day to your selected audience. With this option, you also get the benefits of a Promoted Account campaign.

The given estimate for the benefits from Twitter promote mode is an average additional 30,000 views as well as a net gain of at least 30 new followers per month.

Guide to advertising on Twitter

Getting started: First things first, if you haven't advertised with Twitter before then you will need to set up an account. To do so, all you need to do is to visit ads.Twitter.com and follow the provided instructions.

With that out of the way, you are now ready to choose an objective, in a fashion similar to the process as described in the

Facebook chapter. When it comes to specific options, you can choose from the following:

- Awareness: You want the maximum number of people to see your Promoted tweet. You're billed per 1,000 impressions.
- Tweet engagements: You want to maximize engagement with your Promoted tweets. You're billed per engagement for all engagement types.
- Followers: You want to build your Twitter audience. You're billed for each new follower, but not for other engagements.
- Website clicks or conversions: You want people to go to your website and take action. You're billed per click.
- Promoted video views: You want people to watch your videos or GIFs. You're billed for each video view.
- In-stream video views (pre-roll): You want to run a short video ad at the start of videos from Twitter's premium content partners. You're billed for each video view.

Moving forward: Next you will be taken the screen from which you can create your campaign, give it a name, etc. This is also where you will decide if you wish to start your campaign now or later. You will also set your budget on this screen, either what you wish to spend on the entire campaign, or what you wish to spend per day.

Next, you will need to deal with determining your ad groups, as well as bidding. Unless you are planning to heavily invest in your Twitter marketing you are likely going to want to choose just one group for now to maximize potential engagement. When you first start, however, you may want to consider playing around with timing, targeting different audiences, and the like, to ensure the option you ultimately go with best suits your needs. Should you choose automatic bidding, Twitter will automatically set your bid to get the best results at the lowest price based on your budget.

Select an audience: With the ad options out of the way, you will then choose your target audience in such a way that it serves to maximize your budget. You can target audiences based on language, location, age, and gender. You can target something as broad as a country or as specific as a single zip code. From there, you can get even more specific and determine what types of interests or behaviors you want your target audience to participate in. The Audience Features section will even give you the estimated changes to your audience size for each choice. You also have the option of uploading a predetermined list of individuals.

Launch your campaign: The last step is to review all of your choices and choose the option to Launch campaign to begin. Don't forget to watch your analytics after the fact to ensure you are using your money as effectively as possible.

Quick promote: In addition to the steps above, you can also use the quick promote option. This lets you determine your Twitter ad with just a few clicks. All you do is choose your preferred tweet and your desired audience and it is off to the races.

Conclusion

Thanks for making it through to the end of *Social Media Marketing 2019: How to Become an Influencer of Millions on Facebook, Twitter, Youtube & Instagram While Advertising & Building Your Personal Brand*, let's hope it was informative and able to provide you with all of the tools you need to achieve your goals. Just because you've finished this book doesn't mean there is nothing left to learn on the topic, and expanding your horizons is the only way to find the mastery you seek.

Now that you have made it to the end of this book, you hopefully have an understanding of how to get started building your brand, as well as a strategy or two, or three, that you are anxious to try for the first time. Before you go ahead and start giving it your all, however, it is important that you have realistic expectations as to the level of success you should expect in the near future. Having the wrong expectations this early in the process can lead to situations that feel like failures, even though they are really par for the course. This, in turn, can sour you on a potential marketing avenue, costing you who knows how much over what is essentially a misunderstanding.

Thus it is important to keep in mind that while it is perfectly true that some people experience serious success right out of the gate, it is an unfortunate fact of life that they are the exception rather than the rule. What this means is that you should expect to experience something of a learning curve, especially when you are first figuring out what works for you. This is perfectly normal, however, and if you persevere you will come out the other side better because of it. Instead of getting your hopes up to an unrealistic degree, you should think of your time spent building your brand as a marathon rather than a sprint which means that slow and steady will win the race every single time.

Finally, if you found this book useful in anyway, a review on Amazon is always appreciated!

Made in the USA
Lexington, KY
14 June 2019